Virginia Woolf and the Politics of Language

Virginia Woolf and the Politics of Language

Judith Allen

Edinburgh University Press

First published in hardback by Edinburgh University Press 2010

Edinburgh University Press Ltd
22 George Square, Edinburgh EH8 9LF

www.euppublishing.com

Typeset in 10.5/13 Adobe Sabon
by Servis Filmsetting Ltd, Stockport, Cheshire, and
printed and bound in Great Britain by
CPI Antony Rowe, Chippenham and Eastbourne

A CIP record for this book is available from the British Library

ISBN 978 0 7486 3675 4 (hardback)
ISBN 978 0 7486 6485 6 (paperback)

Contents

Acknowledgements

It is impossible to think about this study without looking back to the Temple University undergraduate class of the late George McFadden, where I was introduced to the writings of both Virginia Woolf and Michel de Montaigne. Disregarding McFadden's advice to major in English literature, I completed a degree in Biology, later returning to graduate school to focus on Virginia Woolf – and to look once more at that book she kept by her bedside, the *Essays* of Michel de Montaigne. Many of the ideas for this book emanated from my work with McFadden, the late Philip Stevick and Alan Wilde, and I look back with gratitude to those productive conversations.

For their support in this effort, my thanks go to copy-editor, Wendy Lee, and desk editor, Eliza Wright. I am especially indebted to Jackie Jones, Head of Publishing at Edinburgh University Press, for her encouragement, patience, and guidance throughout this project.

Acknowledgements for permission to adapt work of my own that has appeared or will appear in print are as follows: (1993), 'Those Soul Mates: Virginia Woolf and Michel de Montaigne', *Virginia Woolf: Themes and Variations, Selected Papers from the Second Annual Conference on Virginia Woolf*, ed. Vara Neverow-Turk and Mark Hussey, and (1999) 'The Rhetoric of Performance in *A Room of One's Own*', *Virginia Woolf and Communities: Selected Papers from the Eighth Annual Conference on Virginia Woolf*, ed. Jeanette McVicker and Laura Davis, copyright granted by Pace University Press, New York; and (2010), 'Virginia Woolf, "Patriotism", and "our prostituted fact-purveyors"', *Virginia Woolf's Bloomsbury*, ed. Lisa Shahriari and Gina Potts, Palgrave Macmillan.

In the course of presenting numerous papers, including those noted above, I have benefited from sharing exciting ideas – and life's ongoing crises – with many friends and colleagues. Particular thanks go to Tuzyline Allan, Pamela Caughie, Krystyna Colburn, Beth Daugherty,

Jeannie Dubino, Lois Gilmore, Evelyn Haller, Mark Hussey, Georgia Johnston, Jane Lilienfeld, Jeanette McVicker, Brenda Silver, Pierre-Eric Villeneuve and J. J. Wilson. It has also been wonderful to be on the receiving end of the boundless generosity of Natalie McKnight, Jane Goldman and Suzanne Bellamy. I thank them.

My 'without whom' is my loving family – Matthew, Lindsay, John, Daniel, grandson Dashiell, and my husband (and chef), Stephen Ward.

For Stephen, Matthew, Lindsay, John, Daniel,
and, especially, Dashiell

Abbreviations

AROO   *A Room of One's Own* ([1929] 1957), New York, NY: Harcourt Brace Jovanovich

AWD   *A Writer's Diary* ([1953] 1973), ed. and intro. Leonard Woolf, New York, NY: Harcourt Brace Jovanovich

BA   *Between the Acts* ([1941] 1969), New York, NY: Harcourt Brace Jovanovich

CDB   *The Captain's Death Bed and Other Essays* (1950), New York, NY: Harcourt Brace Jovanovich

CRI   *The Common Reader: First Series* ([1925] 1984), ed. and intro. Andrew McNeillie, New York, NY: Harcourt Brace Jovanovich

CRII   *The Second Common Reader: Second Series* ([1932] 1986), ed. and intro. Andrew McNeillie, New York, NY: Harcourt Brace Jovanovich

DI–V   *The Diary of Virginia Woolf* (1977–84), ed. Anne Olivier Bell and Andrew McNeillie, 5 vols, New York, NY: Harcourt Brace Jovanovich

DM   *The Death of the Moth and Other Essays* ([1942] 1970), New York, NY: Harcourt Brace Jovanovich

EI–IV   *The Essays of Virginia Woolf* (1986–), ed. Andrew McNeillie, 4 vols, New York, NY: Harcourt Brace Jovanovich

GR   *Granite and Rainbow* ([1958] 1975), New York, NY: Harcourt Brace Jovanovich

JR   *Jacob's Room* ([1922] 1992), ed. and intro. Sue Roe, London: Penguin

LI–VI   *The Letters of Virginia Woolf* (1975–80), ed. Nigel Nicolson and Joanne Trautmann, 6 vols, New York, NY: Harcourt Brace Jovanovich

M   *The Moment and Other Essays* ([1947] 1974), New York, NY: Harcourt Brace Jovanovich

MD   *Mrs Dalloway* ([1925] 1953), New York, NY: Harcourt Brace Jovanovich

MoB   *Moments of Being* (1976), ed. Jeanne Schulkind, New York, NY: Harcourt Brace Jovanovich

ND   *Night and Day* ([1919] 1992), ed. and intro. Julia Briggs, London: Penguin

O   *Orlando* ([1928] 1933), London: Hogarth

P   *The Pargiters: The Novel-Essay Portion of The Years* (1977), ed. and intro. Mitchell A. Leaska, New York, NY: Harcourt Brace Jovanovich

PA   *A Passionate Apprentice* (1990), ed. Mitchell A. Leaska, New York, NY: Harcourt Brace Jovanovich

RN   *Virginia Woolf's Reading Notebooks* (1983), ed. Brenda R. Silver, Princeton, NJ: Princeton University Press

TG   *Three Guineas* ([1938] 1966), New York, NY: Harcourt Brace & World

TTL   *To the Lighthouse* ([1927] 1955), New York, NY: Harcourt Brace

VO   *The Voyage Out* ([1915] 1948), New York, NY: Harcourt Brace & World

W   *The Waves* ([1931] 1959), New York, NY: Harcourt Brace & World

From Michel de Montaigne to the New Media: Reading Virginia Woolf in the Twenty-First Century

Que sais-je?[1]
> Michel de Montaigne, *The Complete Essays of Montaigne*
> Virginia Woolf, 'Montaigne', *The Common Reader*

For language is by no means a perfect vehicle of meanings. Words, like currency, are turned over and over again, to evoke one set of images to-day, another tomorrow. There is no certainty whatever that the same word will call out exactly the same idea in the reader's mind as it did the reporter's.
> Walter Lippmann, *Public Opinion*[2]

My first epigraph, 'Que sais-je?' ['What do I know?'] – used as Montaigne's 'motto' and significantly 'inscribed over a pair of scales' (II:12, 393) – was appropriated by Virginia Woolf as the last line of her essay, 'Montaigne' (*CRI* 68). Reading his *Essays* in English, and eventually in French, she deemed him 'the first of the moderns' in her 1905 essay, 'The Decay of Essay-Writing',[3] and gave him a prominent placement as the first single-author essay in *The Common Reader* in 1925. Woolf's lifelong dialogue with Montaigne, and with the multitude of ancient voices that permeate his *Essays*, enabled her to infuse her own works with commentary about his writing, to compare his methods with those of other writers, and to use his ideas, and his methods, to inspire her future writings. Woolf's veneration of Montaigne prompted her to make three visits – with Leonard – to his Tower in the Dordogne region of France, the place of his creative efforts. Her absolute joy in these visits is evident in her postcards and letters to Vita Sackville-West, Ethel Smyth and Vanessa Bell. Inside the Tower, surrounded by the fifty-seven 'sentences' which Montaigne had painted on the rafters of his library ceiling, Virginia Woolf spoke of 'the very door, room, stairs, and a view precisely the same he saw' (*LIV* 318).[4] The depth of her connection to the individual who created the essay – defined by its indefiniteness, resistant to categorisation or containment, while both expressing and enacting its quest for freedom – underscores his significance in Woolf's life, in her writing practice and, most significantly, in this study. But this complex relationship surely needs further exploration, necessarily keeping in mind the 400 years of separation by language, gender, country and culture, and those contextual aspects that impinge upon our subjects in a multitude of ways but remain elusive. This inquiry will illuminate their shared interests in delineating the complexities of the reading process, the subversion of genre, hierarchies, binary oppositions and the referentiality of language, while privileging contingency, multiple voices, plural subjects, and process over product, and will ultimately show their readers the politics of their language.

Woolf's early attraction to Montaigne's 'essayistic' mode stems from her desire to tamper with genre, to undermine what had been, at the end of the nineteenth century, the 'conventional' novel. With *To the Lighthouse*, she wanted something different from a novel -perhaps 'Elegy?' (*AWD* 78); *The Waves* was to be 'a play-poem' (134); *The Years*, an 'Essay-novel' (183); and *Between the Acts*, a carnivalesque including 'dialogue: and poetry: and prose' (275). And, again subverting genre, *Orlando* (1928) and *Flush* (1933) were mock-biographies. But the 'essayistic', as created by Montaigne – a mode of writing that intersects with other marginalised forms such as diaries, letters, memoirs and autobiography – did not require transformation. Already 'other', hybrid, provisional and resistant to definition, the 'essayistic' both expresses and enacts the inextricable connection between its aesthetics and politics – and given its resistance to all constraints, authorities and totalising systems, it is forever seeking freedom.

Both Woolf and Montaigne – in their writing practice – seem to 'perform' the 'essayistic', a mode of expression that utilises extremely nuanced and complex narrative and rhetorical strategies while inviting the active participation of its readers; their goal is critical thinking. It is also abundantly evident that their writings specifically function – both explicitly and implicitly – to subvert any doctrines, treatises, or constraining and totalising systems. I find myself in agreement with W. Wolfgang Holdheim's assessment of the 'essayistic' project as one that 'opposes experimental soundings to dogmatic reductions and puts *essayistic theorising* in the place of reified theory' (Holdheim 30; emphasis added). For Claire De Obaldia, the 'essayistic' can be applied to 'novels' as well as other genres,[5] and clearly accepts of the mystery and complexity of texts, selves and, most especially, the words from which they are constructed. Words, for Virginia Woolf, must be free of constraints, and in that freedom, as Graham Good points out, 'there is also a sense in the use of "*essayer*," of risk and inconclusiveness, a feeling of venturing outside the paths of conventional methods' (Good 28–9).

This study will roam – in essayistic fashion – on some of those unconventional paths, from the late sixteenth-century Montaigne to the early twentieth-century Woolf, exploring their modes of cultural critique and the relevance of their writings for the twenty-first century. What becomes clear, in the exploration of their narrative and rhetorical strategies, is the current need for critical thinking and a healthy scepticism. The questions provoked by a close examination of their writings, of their theorising of reading and language, will serve to illuminate both the language of politics and the politics of language. Montaigne's seminal question – 'Que sais-je?' – expressing the rampant scepticism of the late sixteenth century, reverberates today, in the first decade of the twenty-first, at a time when we are, quite ironically, inundated with 'information'. At the same time, we are becoming more aware of 'secrecy' as the reigning force in governments around the world – both elected and non-elected – and of the fact that much-needed accountability is non-existent; we are also aware that calls for 'transparency' abound. Both words, 'secrecy' and 'transparency', although seemingly straightforward, are problematic, as Mark Danner points out in his article entitled, 'US Torture: Voices from the Black Sites' (*New York Review of Books*, 9 April 2009): 'And yet, what is "secret" exactly? In our recent politics, "secret" has become an oddly complex word. From whom was "the secret bombing of Cambodia" secret? Not from the Cambodians, surely' (69). Like so many of the words Woolf's *Three Guineas* foregrounds as 'used words' (*TG* 101), words like 'secrecy' and 'transparency', 'information' and 'journalism', and others placed in quotation marks in this study will have to be defined in their immediate context. As Woolf's narrator comments on words and their varied situations in her essay/broadcast 'Craftsmanship', we are reminded that 'they [words] hate anything that stamps them with one meaning or confines them to one attitude, for it is their nature to change':

> It is because the truth they try to catch is many-sided, and they convey it by being themselves many-sided, flashing this way, then that. Thus they mean one thing to one person, another thing to another person; they are unintelligible to one generation, plain as pikestaff to the next. (*DM* 206)

This commentary on language takes us to my second epigraph from Walter Lippmann's landmark study, *Public Opinion* (1922), a text in the library of Leonard and Virginia Woolf. Lippmann, who worked as a propagandist during World War I (WWI) and also as a White House advisor, learned how easy it was to manipulate 'public opinion' – yet another contested term that will play an important part in this study. In his Foreword to a recent edition of *Public Opinion*, Ronald Steel details

the experiences that moved Lippmann to believe that 'distortion of information was inescapable' (xii). Lippmann's assertion was that 'unlike the
pollution of information, whose effects could be sanitized, distortion
was part of the human mind – an essential part. This was because human
beings are creatures not only of reason, but also of emotions, habits, and
prejudices' and that 'how we categorize determines not only how, but
also what we see' (xii). Lippmann 'went beyond [the] simple critique of
press accuracy to pose a more fundamental problem: How could the
public get the information it needed to make rational political judgments
if it could not rely on the press?' (xi). Virginia Woolf, dealing with the
propaganda promulgated during WWI and Britain's problematic media
empire, the Northcliffe Press,[6] was familiar with the manipulation of
language to sell wars, to sell the 'official story'. In *Three Guineas* (1938),
her narrators critique those 'prostituted fact-purveyors', offering prescient advice that clearly resonates with our world today:

> if you want to know any fact about politics, you must read at least three dif-
> ferent newspapers, compare at least three different versions of the same fact,
> and come in the end to your own conclusion. . . . In other words, you have to
> strip each statement of its money motive, of its power motive, of its advertise-
> ment motive, of its publicity motive . . . before you make up your mind about
> which fact of politics to believe. (*TG* 95)[7]

Given that we also try to decide 'which fact of politics to believe', the
need for critical thinking, for an awareness of how language is used by
those in power to persuade, to gain market share, to forge ahead with
agendas that enable them to create and/or ignore the people's voices, is
more important than ever – especially given the global economic crisis of
2008, the decision-making process for beginning the war in Iraq, and the
realisation that we simply do not have enough 'information'. Woolf's
narrator calls attention to the 'facts of politics', continues her interrogation of 'facts' and suggests that there are clearly 'different versions of the
same fact' (*TG* 95).

The words 'secrecy' and 'transparency', along with 'torture', 'post-
traumatic stress disorder', 'drones', 'indefinite detention' and 'Abu
Ghraib' – to name just a few – are now part of the lexicon of our twenty-
first-century lives, as the words 'bomb', 'landmine', 'civilian' and 'photographs of dead bodies and ruined houses' (*TG* 141) – all mentioned
in the writings of Virginia Woolf – are still with us, still haunting our
lives, with new additions and videos etched in our minds. It is difficult
not to think of the words of lexicographer Eric Partridge: 'War is a powerful excitant, perhaps the most rapidly effectual excitant, of language.
It quickens and enlivens, enriches and invigorates language as much in

the twentieth century as exploration and travel used to do in the 16th-17th centuries.' [8] Interestingly, the words he uses – 'quicken', 'enlivens', 'enriches' and 'invigorates' – all linked with life, emanate from that harbinger of torture and death, war. Geoffrey Hughes has assessed changes in the language of war over the centuries, and explores the new lexicon of war in the twenty-first century – with the familiar 'weapons of mass destruction' (WMD), 'shock and awe', and 'mission accomplished' – while older Orwellian euphemisms ensure that 'the ministries of *war* have been restyled ministries of *defence*' (Hughes 16). And with a nod to Hollywood movies, Chris Hedges, a former war correspondent for *The New York Times*, finds that the suicide bombers of 9/11 'learned that huge explosions and death above a city skyline are a peculiar and effective form of communication. They have mastered the language' (Hedges 8). Hedges also points out that 'the adoption of the cause means adoption of the language of the cause. When we speak within the confines of this language we give up our linguistic capacity to question and make moral choices' (148).

Like war, nothing draws more attention to the manipulation of language than a lengthy political campaign. As the world watched and read the minute-by-minute coverage of Barack Obama's campaign for the presidency of the US, his words called forth strong emotional responses – especially his promises of 'transparency', frequently used in his speeches to undermine the Bush Administration's culture of deception. That promised 'transparency', a word that has clearly been overused, is now proving increasingly opaque, as organisations such as Transparency International and the Sunlight Foundation escalate their investigations into government and corporate fraud – inextricably connected with one another – as well as war crimes, environmental and non-environmental disasters, warrantless wiretapping and other pressing matters.[9] Encouraged by the beliefs, now widely held but certainly not new, across the political spectrum – that 'information' is likely to be 'disinformation', that material is being selectively withheld from the public – Montaigne's question, 'Que sais-je?', now recontextualised and propelled by much anger, is centre-stage in many countries; this is evident from the 2009 Chilcot Inquiry[10] into the UK's decisions regarding the country's involvement in the Iraq War. We are intermittently reminded that things have been concealed, that there is much we do not know, as we witness what surfaces from the past. Most recently, in August 2009, Daniel Ellsberg, who leaked the 'Pentagon Papers' in 1971 by revealing classified US documents about the Vietnam War to *The New York Times* and other newspapers, began a project to reveal information that had been concealed from the world since 1945, regarding the horrific bombings of Hiroshima and Nagasaki. This is material from sixty-four years ago that is finally being revealed.[11] It is impossible to know what has been hidden from us – or what continues to be concealed, rebranded or euphemistically renamed, thus gaining public acceptance.

With so many countries struggling with 'fundamentalisms', human rights violations', the stifling of dissent, government/corporate control of the media, and – in many instances – the electoral process, we also note the failure of that crucial tool of democracy, an independent press. Given the continual expansion of this situation, there is a need for scepticism, critical thinking and, ultimately, a greater understanding of the complexities of language. We currently live in a world of 'spin', 'sound bites' and 'strategic leaks' – in constant supply by governments, corporations, and designated 'pundits' spread across the political spectrum – all disseminated in real time by both the 'mainstream media' and the 'new media' outlets, with each contending for a specific audience. At the turn of the twentieth century and in its early years, Virginia Woolf had access to a multitude of newspapers and magazines, as well as radio, photography and cinema; today we add the burgeoning 'new media' of Twitter, Facebook, e-mail, text messages, YouTube and at least 133 million 'blogs'[12] at the time of writing. Individuals around the world, those with the economic means to link up to the Internet, are faced with increasingly complex problems regarding issues of censorship and/or privacy, and most importantly, the extreme difficulty of trying to ascertain the sources of this 'information', the validity, the reliability, the inherent bias of what has now become an instantaneous onslaught of words, parts of words, photos and videos. The questions take on an Orwellian tone: Where does this 'information' originate? Who controls it? What has been left out? And with all that is available – across this broad political spectrum – how do we whittle down the possibilities, decide which blogs to read and choose what sources to place on our 'home page'? Is our necessarily skewed selection beneficial? Do we read the 'opposing voices' with any degree of openness? And what about 'citizen journalism'?[13] Is everyone eligible? How do we interpret the Twitter communication that supposedly enabled the world to 'know' what was happening during the recent election protest in Iran on 12 June 2009 (*Time.com*, 12 June 2009)?

With the mainstream press so embedded in the corporations that own them, there are concerns that these media outlets will – or have already become – indistinguishable from the voices of their corporate owners. Revelations that the US Pentagon hired retired generals to appear on CNN and other mainstream news outlets to deliver military propaganda (*The New York Times*, 22 April 2008) provide reason for concern,[14] as do the earlier apologies (buried in the back of the paper) from *The New York Times* and *The Washington Post* after they chose to echo the Bush Administration's 'talking points' and policies during the lead-up to the Iraq War, and the willingness of *The New York Times* to withhold significant news stories at the request of the Bush Administration[15]. The 'progressive' press – television shows like *GRITtv*, *Democracy Now* and *Bill Moyers' Journal* in the US, and journals such as *The Nation* and *Harper's Magazine*, as well as *Mother Jones*, *The New York Review of Books* and the *London Review of Books*, to name but a few – along with many blogs and newsletters from the 'new media', have become our resident 'outsiders', the watchdogs of democracy, the voices of the voiceless; they are sometimes joined by Libertarians, and some from the right wing of American politics, along with a few courageous military figures who have resigned to protest against official policies.[16]

Unfortunately, most people get their news from 'sound bites' of the mainstream press, while, quite fortunately, a certain segment of the population supplements its 'news' with sources from around the world, and from the comedy programme, *The Daily Show with Jon Stewart*. The latter, although appearing on the *Comedy Central* network, owned by a major media corporation, *Viacom*, is known as a 'comedy' show; despite – or perhaps because of – this, it is able to address very significant issues, sometimes in a very serious way, without causing major marketing concerns. Perhaps this is the power of 'genre', the power of the label 'comedy', that denies its seriousness to a certain segment of the population, thus enabling this show to speak quite seriously to its own progressive audience. Many serious journalists in both the mainstream press and the new media make reference to the political opinions voiced by Jon Stewart, often questioning why such astute commentary comes to us via 'comedy'. Another show on *Comedy Central*, *The Colbert Report*, a mock 'conservative' news programme, is also responsible for bringing a segment called 'The Word' to its large audience; in its oblique way it serves to foreground the difficulties of our language in the context of its comedic framework. Bringing back the word 'truthiness' in 2005 – named 'Word of the Year' by the American Dialect Association in 2005 and by Merriam-Webster in 2006 – the show focuses its audience's attention on the varied concepts of 'truth', concepts that both Montaigne and Woolf viewed with increasing scepticism. The words 'truthy' and 'truthiness' appear in the *Oxford English Dictionary* (*OED*) with a citation from 1824, with both referring to 'truthfulness'. This definition has now been transformed by its new satirical meaning: 'a "truth" that a person claims to know intuitively, *from the gut*, without regard to evidence, logic, intellectual examination or facts' (Dick Meyer, 'The Truth of Truthiness', CBS News, 14 December 2006).[17] Montaigne, Bakhtin and Woolf would probably go with 'truthiness', given their resistance to dictionary definitions and their scepticism regarding 'truth'.

Attention to language is extremely important today, as our level of trust rapidly diminishes. When we read what is considered 'news', we should clearly be focused on the words that are chosen. Are we dealing with 'torture' or 'enhanced interrogation techniques'? Did the bombs kill 'civilians' and 'noncombatants', or are these people simply considered to be 'collateral damage'? Just how long will the 'indefinite detention' of detainees from Iraq, called for by the Obama Administration (*New York Times*, 21 May 2009), last – and whatever happened to 'due process'? In David Bromwich's excellent article, 'Euphemism and American Violence' (*New York Review of Books*, 3 April 2008), he reminds his readers of the famous sentence from Tacitus' *Agricola*:[18] 'To robbery, butchery, and rapine, they give the lying name of "government"; they create a desolation and call it peace.' According to Bromwich: 'The frightening thing about such acts of renaming or *euphemism*, Tacitus implies, is their power to efface the memory of actual cruelties. Behind the façade of a history falsified by language, the painful particulars of war are lost' (Bromwich 28). Noting that 'one extreme of euphemism comes from naturalizing the cruelties of power, the opposite extreme arises from a nerve-deadening understatement' of George Orwell's 'Politics and the English Language':

> Defenceless villages are bombarded from the air, the inhabitants driven out into the countryside, the cattle machine-gunned, the huts set on fire with incendiary bullets: this is called *pacification*. Millions of peasants are robbed of their farms and sent trudging along the roads with no more than they can carry: this is called *transfer of population or rectification of frontiers*. People are imprisoned for years without trial, or shot in the back of the neck or sent to die of scurvy in Arctic lumber camps: this is called *elimination of unreliable elements*. Such phraseology is needed if one wants to name things without calling up mental pictures of them. (28; Bromwich's emphasis)

As we have been inundated with revelations about 'Black sites', 'extraordinary rendition', repeated videos of 'water-boarding', and photos from 'Abu Ghraib', there is a countermove, as Bromwich asserts, to change the language for the purpose of deception. For Bromwich, this kind of complacency is 'the correlative in moral psychology of euphemism in the realm of language' (30). Both *The New York Times* and National Public Radio (NPR) refused, until late in 2009, to use the word 'torture',[19] finding 'enhanced interrogation techniques' quite satisfactory; the formation of NPR Check was a response to what many in the media considered the euphemising of 'torture'.

Given the difficulties of ascertaining what is happening today, how much has changed since Virginia Woolf was confronted with the propaganda of the Northcliffe Press? Will corporatism win out regarding its control of the dissemination of 'information', 'packaging and selling candidates', and the 'creation of brands, amongst so many other controls'? Paraphrasing Virginia Woolf's essay, 'How Should One Read a Book?', one might ask: How should one read any writing today, at the close of the first decade of the twenty-first century? The narrator's concerns in Woolf's essay revolve around her readers' abilities to accept a few ideas and suggestions regarding reading, but most importantly, to make certain that these readers will ultimately have the power to resist authorities, and 'not allow them to fetter that independence which is the most important quality that a reader can possess' (*CRII* 258). These readers, we are told, may 'attempt to make something as formed and controlled as a building: but words are more impalpable than bricks; reading is a longer and more complicated process than seeing' (259). Virginia Woolf's astute commentary on the impalpability of words, theorised in her essay, 'Craftsmanship', pervades the corpus of her writings and resoundingly asserts that 'words do not live in dictionaries, they live in the mind' (204, 205). These changeable 'words' resist being 'stamped with one meaning, or confined to one attitude' (206), for they – anthropomorphised here and in so many of Woolf's texts – seek freedom. Always writing about writing, about language, Woolf's varied texts – essays, novels, short stories, diaries, letters – express and enact her political vision, as her readers, unsettled and potentially transformed by their individual interactions with her complex narrative and rhetorical strategies, are positioned to revise their thinking, while inevitably co-creating the texts.

My overall goal for this study is to acknowledge the relevance of Virginia Woolf's writing to our increasingly complex problems regarding the reception of language. Her theorisation of language, I will argue, is fully integrated into the critique offered to her readers; aware of the inadequacies of language and the complexities of the reading process, as well as the readers' conscious and unconscious motivations, her narrator's call for scepticism applies to the 'facts' themselves, as well as the modes disseminating these 'facts'. Woolf prompts her readers to ask significant questions: who controls the language, what are the discernible motivations, and which government official, corporation, or media empire might 'burke discussion of any undesirable subject' (*TG* 162)?

My study will approach Virginia Woolf as a writer theorising language, one who looks back to Montaigne's theorising of language, his extremely modern concepts of reading that language, while she simultaneously interrogates the risks and dangers of reading, writing and being a theorist. I will, as Woolf – and M. M. Bakhtin – did, look back to Montaigne, focusing not only on what he says he is doing, but what he is actually doing; Woolf will require a similar approach. Considered 'one of the earliest philosophic architects of modern liberal politics' (Schaefer, David L. 76), Montaigne created a mode of writing that both expresses and enacts resistance and freedom. Implicitly subversive and defined by its indefiniteness, the essay – always hybrid and 'other' – displays a propensity for engagement; it also functions, according to Theodor Adorno, to 'resist the idea of the master-work' for 'its totality . . . is that of non-totality' (165). Woolf's theorising of language comes out of a similar resistance to fixed categories, whether genres, gender, characters, or the very words that construct them. Although several critics have assessed the varied connections between Montaigne and Woolf (see Judith Allen, Juliet Dusinberre, Nicola Luckhurst and Dudley Marchi), my expanded examination of Woolf's lifelong dialogue with his *Essays*, with close readings of essays by both Montaigne and Woolf, will serve to reveal Montaigne's pervasive presence in her works.

The first of my three sections will explore Montaigne and Woolf as writers who self-consciously theorise reading and language. My first chapter will document, through reading notes, letters, diary entries, essays and her essay/novel, *The Pargiters*, Woolf's lifelong relationship with Montaigne. In investigating the politics of the 'essayistic 'mode of expression as it has been explored by Adorno, Lukács, De Obaldia, Pater, Friedrich, Cave, Deleuze and others, and close intertextual readings of essays by Montaigne and Woolf, interestingly intruded upon by Bakhtin, I hope to make Montaigne's writings – not very often taught today – more familiar. Chapter 2 will examine Woolf's essay/radio broadcast, 'Craftsmanship', which begins with an interrogation of its own title. After a close reading of Woolf's most significant work about 'words', I will discuss the intricacies of choosing and reading 'titles', and examine the progression of 'titles' Woolf created for so many of her works.

The second section, 'The Politics of Writing', will investigate Woolf's narrative and rhetorical strategies, showing how her use of single words, in varied forms and constantly recontextualised, functions metaphorically to make a political statement. In Chapter 3, I will focus, as Woolf does, on the word 'but', used in self-conscious fashion in *A Room of One's Own*, as well as many other texts, to interrupt, to establish the contradictory aspects of differing voices, differing arguments, to hold several ideas in place while assessing their validity, or simply to resist any final judgement. In Chapter 4, I utilise Hayden White's *Tropics of Discourse*, a study that examines the survival of the word 'wildness', in its dialectical relations to 'civilisation'; I re-read Woolf's many metaphorical references to the 'wild' through the lens of Montaigne's 'Of Cannibals', an essay well known to Woolf. I will also explore aspects of sixteenth-century colonialism as depicted in Montaigne's essay, 'Of Coaches', for what he voices resonates with Woolf's views on colonialism as they are expressed in *The Voyage Out*. Most importantly, I will explore Woolf's appropriation of 'wildness' for women, as it is expressed and enacted by her writing, and, most especially, by the 'wildness' that acts as a necessary mode of resistance to both the exclusionary and the coercive tactics of 'civilisation', as depicted and confronted in their lives.

The third section will focus on 'Dialogue and Dissent', with Chapter 5 examining the importance of dialogue, of all modes of 'conversation', as exemplified by Woolf's 'essayistic' practice and the very process of reading. That Virginia Woolf liked 'to be in the position of the one asked' (*DIV* 361) is significant here, as she does not want to dictate to her readers; in this context, I will show how, in setting up complex conversations, varied voices are heard and differing perspectives are provided. I will focus on the language and the interactions of 'Thoughts on Peace in an Air Raid', a work written in 1940 and extremely relevant to our current world situation. This work will also provide an opportunity to talk about the language of war – in Woolf's time and our own – the 'subconscious Hitlerism' (*DM* 245) assessed by Woolf's narrator, and the relevance of the arguments expressed by this essay for the women of the twenty-first century, as it is read today in the context of Iraq, Afghanistan, Pakistan, Gaza, Somalia, Congo, Indonesia, India and so many other war zones. It also calls forth a discussion about women's place at the various 'tables' in our world, about women's voices in times of war and potential acts of resistance.

Chapter 6 will explore patriotism and newspapers, in Woolf's time and our own. As we re-read Virginia Woolf's *Three Guineas* in 2009, permeated as it is by repeated references to 'patriotism', 'prostituted fact-purveyors' and 'photographs of dead bodies and ruined houses', we are deeply saddened by the familiarity of it all – and perhaps outraged that this text is so very relevant today. I will address that relevancy, and focus on what happens to those who dare to 'think against the current' – and more problematic, to 'speak against the current', an issue still problematic for women and all 'outsiders' today.

Viewing our modern world, as the first decade of the twenty-first century comes to a close, I will focus on the relevance of Woolf's mode of writing, her ideas regarding language, and the importance of how we read that language. I will demonstrate how Woolf shows her readers the importance of critical thinking in a world where uncertainty reigns, where so-called democracies are insidiously dismantled, human rights are lost, coercive practices continue, dissent is silenced, and simply reading the 'words' placed before us has become a daunting task. Woolf's writings, and those of Montaigne before her, point to the need for critical thinking, for becoming active participants in accessing information. Her modes of expression work toward that result. In this exploration of the 'essayistic', with its focus on engagement, interaction and critique, we will not necessarily gain any definitive answers, but in its function as a mode of cultural critique, Woolf's mode of expression provides an opportunity for diverse voices to be heard. Given the explosion of 'new media', 'knowing' what is happening in our ever-shrinking world has become more complicated than ever. Yet the question with which I began should remain in our minds today: 'Que-sais-je?'

Notes

1. Michel de Montaigne (1965), 'Apology for Raymond Sebond', *The Complete Essays of Montaigne*, trans. Donald M. Frame, Stanford, CA: Stanford University Press, 393. Montaigne called what I have used as my epigraph his motto and had it made into a medal with a pair of scales beneath; on the other side it said in Greek: 'I abstain.' In Virginia Woolf's essay, 'Montaigne', his motto is written 'Que scais-je?' (*CRI* 68).
2. This is from Walter Lippmann's *Public Opinion* (1922), a work that was in the library of Leonard and Virginia Woolf. Leonard had met him on a train and they discussed Freud. Lippmann's work as a propagandist during World War I, and in the US Government, influenced his provocative book.
3. Woolf refers to Montaigne as 'the first of the moderns' in her 1905 essay, 'The Decay of Essay-Writing'. This was her first publication in *The Guardian*, the journal of a religious organisation and not the newspaper, and is collected in (1986–) *The Essays of Virginia Woolf*, vol. 1, 24–7.
4. In Terence Cave's excellent article, 'Problems of Reading in the *Essais*', he speaks of Montaigne's love of quotation, and notes that in his *Essays* he has quotations from Greek, Latin, French and Italian, which seem like 'foreign bodies' in his text. There are more than 1,300 quotations in the *Essays*, which were composed between 1572 and 1590 in Montaigne's Tower in the Dordogne. Woolf visited with Leonard Woolf in 1931, 1937 and 1938, and has written about these trips in her letters and diaries. These visits will be discussed in Chapter 1.
5. See Claire De Obaldia (1995), *The Essayistic Spirit: Literature, Modern Criticism, and the Essay*, Oxford: Clarendon, 23–34.

6. The media empire of Woolf's day, the Northcliffe Press, was founded by Alfred Harmsworth in 1888, with magazines and then a chain of newspapers, and invented the modern British newspaper, founding the *Daily Mail* and the *Daily Mirror*, and buying *The Times*. Very knowledgeable about advertising, Harmsworth soon found himself a propagandist in later years. According to biographer, Paul Ferris, 'The Harmsworths caught and distilled into print the spirit of a guilt-free, imperialist Britain, loving every minute of its power' (4). Harmsworth became Lord Northcliffe, amongst his many titles.

7. I want to thank Pamela Caughie for reminding me of this wonderfully prescient passage from *Three Guineas*.

8. Attributed to British lexicographer, Eric Partridge (1894–1979).

9. Founded in 1993, www.transparency.org is a global society with a mission to fight corruption; www.sunlight.com was formed in 2006 and seeks to explore corruption in the US Congress. Other 'watchdog' groups, such as www.factcheck.org, www.fair.org and www.mediamatters.org/transparency, are simply a few examples of this fairly new enterprise.

10. The Chilcot Inquiry, announced in June 2009 by British Prime Minister, Gordon Brown, was to investigate the UK's role in the Iraq War. At first meant to be conducted via closed hearings, that decision was reversed. The results were to be announced by June 2010.

11. The break-in at Ellsberg's psychiatrist's office became part of Watergate, and the ensuing investigation eventually led to the resignation of President Richard Nixon.

12. According to Arianna Huffington of the blog, *Huffington Post*, there were 112 million blogs in 2008, this figure increasing substantially each year. Other sources cite higher numbers, such as *Technorati*, who claim the figure is 133 million and growing.

13. The motto, 'Every Citizen is a Reporter', was coined in 2000 by Oh Yeon Ho, for his South Korean site, http://english.ohmynews.com/. Jay Rosen, of the New York University School of Journalism, defines 'citizen journalism' thus: 'When the people formerly known as the audience employ the press tools they have in their possession to inform one another, that's *citizen journalism*' (PressThink). Jay Rosen chose 'PressThink' instead of 'MediaThink' for his blog because he wants to keep the word 'press' alive; he likes that one fights for 'freedom of the press'.

14. Retired generals, many with ties to the 'defence industry', were hired to present the Pentagon's 'talking points' to the public on CNN and other major mainstream and cable stations. This was a front-page story in *The New York Times* on 22 April 2008. These retired generals were gone from TV for several years but, as of December 2009, they apparently are back to push the Pentagon's agenda.

15. *New York Times* editor, Bill Keller, withheld important information at the behest of the Bush Administration, due to the story's potentially damaging effects just before the election. Keller withheld the story for fourteen months, although he first said it was one year. That additional time, and that information, might have made a difference to the voting public and potentially a difference in the election results. *The New York Times* had made this mistake before, when it became the voice of the government

and not the voice of the people. See (2006), 'The Public Editor', *The New York Times* (1 Jan).

16. Major Ho, a former Marine Corps captain, became the first US official to resign in protest over the Afghan War.

17. *The Colbert Report*, on *Comedy Central*, is a fake news, commentary and talk show that also pretends to be politically far-right.

18. In David Bromwich's (2008) article on euphemism in the *New York Review of Books*, he references Tacitus' *Agricola* (written c. 98 AD), in which the writer talks about his father-in-law, a Roman general and historian.

19. *The New York Times* and NPR were recently in the news for refusing to use the word 'torture' during their broadcasts. They preferred 'harsh interrogation techniques'. See Glen Greenwald at *Salon.com*.

Part I

'Theorising' Reading, 'Theorising' Language

Chapter 1

Those Soul Mates: Virginia Woolf and Michel de Montaigne

> Reading is an intimate act, perhaps more intimate than any other human act. I say that because of the prolonged (or intense) exposure of one mind to another that is involved in it, and because it is the level of mind at which feelings and hopes are dealt in by consciousness and words. . . . If the reader is not at risk, he is not reading. And if the writer is not at risk, he is not writing.
>
> Harold Brodkey, 'Reading is the Most Dangerous Game', *The New York Times Book Review*[1]

Risk. Danger. These are certainly not the words that come to mind when thinking about reading and writing, nor the pangs of anxiety one tends to associate with these words. But the writings of the late sixteenth-century Michel de Montaigne and the early twentieth-century Virginia Woolf express and enact the significance of the intimacy between reader and writer – between reader and text. Both were intensely interested in what ensues when one brings one's self, in all its mystery and mutability, to meet another self, as it is embodied in their carefully chosen words and punctuation, deftly arranged on the page. What is the risk of following a mind moving along varying trajectories, venturing to places unknown? It suggests a voyage for both writer and reader, taking both to uncharted territories. The words they encounter dredge up unconscious scenarios, produce physiological responses, and provoke many feelings that simply defy anticipation or control. This complex interaction somehow produces 'meaning' – for that reader, at that moment and in that particular place. It may be transformative, simply provoke a state of denial, or stimulate any number of mysterious responses.

In this chapter, in the process of establishing the intricate and special relationship that Woolf had with Montaigne's *Essays* throughout her life, and their focus on the complex interactions between reader and writer, I will look back to the beginnings, to Woolf's early exposure to Montaigne's writings, her interest in and admiration of the writers of the

Renaissance, and other authors influenced by Montaigne's work. I will also explore how the 'essayistic', significantly defined by its indefiniteness, its potential wildness and its function as cultural critique, became 'the unsettled ground' for a study of Virginia Woolf and the politics of language.

Questions abound. How do readers make judgements about writing, about writers, about words and how they function? How do readers respond to the internalised voices of authorities, critics and the multitudinous experiences that potentially impinge upon these judgements? Are they conscious of these voices? These complex acts – reading and writing – encourage individuals to take a stand, to make difficult choices. For writers, this involves selecting and arranging words, risking exposure, with no option of erasure; for the reader, these words may provoke new emotions, precipitate life-changing events, and with each new reading offer an infinitely different experience.

Montaigne and Woolf were voracious readers and frequently assessed the writings of others while simultaneously reflecting back on their own work. The printing press arrived in Paris in 1469, and by the 1580s Montaigne's library, in his Tower in the Dordogne, held a thousand volumes, an unusually high number for that era. Both writers kept 'reading notes' on all of their copious readings, later using that material for their 'essayistic' renderings. Virginia Woolf's father, Leslie Stephen, as an essayist and the editor of the *Dictionary of National Biography*,[2] enabled her to access many well-known writers. As her teacher and mentor, Stephen provided her with the literary milieu from which she could appropriate – or reject – the history, biography, philosophy and classical writings freely available to her from his library. This opportunity, however, did not make up for her exclusion from the Cambridge education made available to her brothers, and her writings express her anger about that situation. As Jane Fisher suggests, Woolf's socialisation as a British middle-class woman was controlled by Stephen, and he became the *pater familias* against whom she had to rebel, as well as the liberal intellectual writer and thinker she needed as a mentor (Fisher 33). Leslie Stephen's teachings were often adapted to Woolf's own needs, as in the case of his strong beliefs that 'writers had to be placed in their social and political contexts,' and his insistence that 'texts such as letters, diaries, and state papers were as crucial to understanding literary and cultural history as fiction or poetry' (Silver, *Gender of Modernism* 651). But, as Silver states, 'Where Woolf differs is in transforming these writings, considered even by Stephen to be of secondary importance, into primary inscriptions of women's creativity' (651). In her essay on her father, 'Leslie Stephen' (1932), Woolf speaks of 'the right to think one's own thoughts and to follow one's own pursuits', and suggests that 'no one respected and indeed insisted upon freedom more completely than he did' (*CDB* 74). But Woolf's ambivalence toward Leslie Stephen was clearly expressed in many of her essays. For her, this 'godlike, yet childlike' individual saw his world as 'black and white'; and it was also a world where 'domestic virtues' were to be preserved (*MoB* 113, 115). Fisher points to Woolf's consistent attempts to challenge these binaries of that era: 'between intellect and social gossip, experience and purity, male and female, mind and body – that structured her development' (Fisher 34). Paradoxically, Stephen's encouragement of Woolf's intellectual powers enabled her to criticise his unacceptable behaviour.

Leslie Stephen's early instructions to the young Virginia Stephen – to trust her own judgement when reading literature – are clearly echoed by a narrator in Woolf's essay, 'How Should One Read a Book?' This much quoted advice, to 'come to your own conclusions' (*CRII* 258), reflects her father's advice to her, as she perused the books he purchased specifically for her, and, as she relates in 'Leslie Stephen', 'allowing a girl of 15 the free run of a large and unexpurgated library' (*CDB* 74). But one must also acknowledge her ambivalence regarding her relationship with her father. This is quite clear in the diary entry of 28 November 1928:

> 1928
> Father's birthday. He would have been   1832 96, yes,
>   96
> today; & could have been 96, like other people one has known; but mercifully was not. His life would have entirely ended mine. What would have happened? No writing, no books; inconceivable. (*DIII* 208)

Woolf's initial assessment, that his living would have meant her death – the end of her writing life – is immediately qualified by a question, then a return to her deathlike expectation – 'no writing, no books' – and her final answer to herself: 'inconceivable'. This diary entry echoes the kind of dialogic thinking, the oscillatory mode, found in both Montaigne's and Woolf's 'essayistic' writings, filled as they are with contradictions, questions, multiple narrators and many quotations. She does, however, have some doubts about dialogue, and in a letter to R. C. Trevelyan of 20 April 1934 she voices those questions and makes a suggestion. Sensing something restricting in dialogue, she wants a 'less formed, more natural medium'. What she suggests, however, is not something different from dialogue, but a 'dialogue between different parts of yourself perhaps, now, at this moment' (*LV* 293–4). Her goal with this dispersion of subjectivity is not simply a resistance to an authoritarian stance, although that is certainly present, but it also involves access to the multiple selves that contribute to the protean selves that we are; and specifying 'this moment' acknowledges both the complexities of context as well as the transitory self.

Readers over the years have struggled with the exceptionally intricate narrative and rhetorical strategies of both Montaigne and Woolf, strategies that express and enact the inextricable connection between their aesthetics and politics, but may not be readily perceptible to their readers. Consciously and unconsciously, that seems to be part of their strategy. Focusing on the complicated processes of reading and writing, while simultaneously providing a running commentary on their own writing, they create a sometimes uncomfortable situation for their readers. Their 'essayistic' writings function as cultural critique, as their readers assess their frequently contradictory views; during this process, readers attempt to decipher these intricate arguments, while seeking to establish their own views. Their writings have led many to view Montaigne's and Woolf's provisional assessments as 'theories', and, in the process, to view Montaigne and Woolf as 'theorists'. As a word, 'theorist', with its multitudinous meanings, too often conjures up definitions that align this term with systematising, with a rigidity that precludes any creative spirit; in the context of the writings of Montaigne and Woolf, this not only becomes an extremely problematic label, but, interestingly, it also reflects one of the central concerns of this study.

To return to my epigraph, perhaps 'theorising' about reading and language – or more accurately, positing that Virginia Woolf and Michel de Montaigne are 'theorists' of reading and language – may also be fraught with danger. Both writers would in all likelihood contest this label, question its function, its validity, and with a modicum of equivocation, suggest something infinitely more applicable. After convincing readers of the effectiveness of their newly ambiguous identity, they would, perhaps – definitely using the word 'perhaps' – attempt to undermine it. Other contradictory options might be offered, but nothing conclusive would be forthcoming. And yet, despite this imagined scene of mutual protestation at the 'theorist' label, the writings of Montaigne and Woolf most assuredly express and enact a pervasive interest in the problematics of reading and writing – and, ultimately, in the inadequacies of language. As writers whose writings work to resist doctrines, hierarchies, abstractions, stasis and all totalising systems, the word 'theory', when applied to their works, conjures up much that these two writers spent their writing lives subverting.

Many scholars of the 'essay' have weighed in on the problem of 'theorising' and the 'essayistic', relating it to debates revolving around 'fragmentary versus totalising modes of thought – between essay and system'

(Kauffmann 232),[3] and Montaigne's view on this subject is, ironically, quite definitive: 'I do not see the whole of anything,' and 'nor do those who promise to show it to us' (I:50, 219). Montaigne's tentative method of experiencing the world does not have 'a logical intent', for when he speaks of 'distinguishing', he refers to 'a distinguishing of uncategorizable facts, [and] means a differentiating view that increases the variety of what is observed through the change in viewpoint' (Friedrich 153). This connects with Graham Good's assessment of 'theorising', and its relation to reading the *Essays* of Montaigne: 'what the Montaignean essay demands of the reader is not passive assent to a set of propositions or to a body of doctrine, but his active engagement' (Good 163). John A. McCarthy, investigating the essay during the eighteenth century, finds that 'the searing inquisitiveness characteristic of essayistic style is akin to the method of philosophical skepticism prevalent in the Enlightenment' (McCarthy 7). And Montaigne's 'theory', as viewed by Terence Cave, is 'so intermittent, so deliberately unsystematic, that to attempt to make of it a coherent structure of thought would be to ignore and falsify the character of his discourse' (Cave 134).

Virginia Woolf's 1940 essay, 'The Leaning Tower', continuing her lifelong interest in illuminating the problematics of writing and reading, begins with an interrogation of the 'theorising' of those subjects. Starting with a definitive statement meant to keep its readers 'steady on [their] path', it depicts a writer who 'keeps his eye *fixed*, as *intently* as he can, upon a *certain* object'. The narrator, aligned with the reader and clearly not 'steady', quickly finds that 'the writer has to keep his eye upon a model that *moves*, that *changes*, upon an object that is *not one* object but *innumerable* objects.' Ultimately, the reader is told that 'two words alone cover all that a writer looks at – they are, "human life"' (*M* 128; emphasis mine). No two words could be more inscrutable or more open to interpretation, and, therefore, no two words will better serve Woolf's purpose. Her narrator feels compelled to inform the readers that 'at present we have only theories about writers – a great many theories.' And not surprisingly, 'they all differ.' These 'differing theories' – from 'politicians', 'artists', 'psychologists' and 'genealogists' – are then proffered as evidence, with the narrator deducing that we are not only 'in the dark about writers', but clearly, 'anybody can make a theory.' And with further undermining: 'the germ of the theory is almost always the wish to prove what the theorist wishes to believe.' Informed that 'theories . . . are dangerous things,' we are also told that 'we must risk making one this afternoon since we are going to discuss modern tendencies,' and given that these tendencies are influential, 'we must then have a theory as to what this influence is. But let us always remember – influences are infinitely numerous; writers are infinitely sensitive; each writer has different sensibility. That is why literature is always changing, like the weather, like the clouds in the sky' (*M* 128–300). And so the theorising, the questioning of theorising – and the eventual undermining of 'theorising' – is set before the reader, as the 'theorising' continues unabated.

For both Montaigne and Woolf, there is a need for a new kind of writing, one that does not separate theory from practice; what is needed, according to W. Wolfgang Holdheim's assessment of Montaigne, is a counter-practice that may function as a counter-statement: one that opposed experimental sounding to dogmatic reductions and puts essayistic theorising in the place of reified theory' (Holdheim 30). I too would relate Montaigne's (and Woolf's)'theorising' to 'essaying', and find that *'essayistic theorising'* expresses their reliance on experience, on feelings, and on the linkage of mind and body; it also must involve, as Holdheim points out, 'an acceptance of the risk of uncertainty' (24; emphasis added). It is important to note that this mode of expression, the 'essayistic', does apply to Woolf's other writings, and most notably to many of her novels. As Claire De Obaldia asserts in her study, *The Essayistic Spirit*, 'the "essayistic" can be applied to novels, poems, plays' for 'the novel seems to rise from the essay' (De Obaldia 20, 16).

> In the works of Barthes and Bakhtin, in fact, what I have described as the 'essayistic' or 'essayism' is presented as 'novelistic' or 'novelness,' and is associated with the indeterminacy, open-endedness, and generic criticism typical of the progressive, boundless, and non-canonic genre of the novel. (De Obaldia 24)

But Woolf, of course, in her tampering with genre, truly transformed her later novels, made them hybrid modes, and rendered their generic qualities uncertain. This essayistic 'uncertainty', conveyed by the narrative and rhetorical strategies of both Woolf and Montaigne, enables readers to see multiple viewpoints, differing angles and oscillating opinions, while prompting these participatory readers to think critically, to read critically, and to ensure, with this healthy scepticism, the freedom to come to a conclusion or to conclude that no conclusion is possible.

My exploration of the 'essayistic' will show its inherent resistance to any definition of 'theory' or 'theorising' that encompasses a systematising or totalising concept, for everything about the essay subverts these constraints and limitations. In his excellent commentary on the subject of 'reading' in Montaigne's *Essays*, Terence Cave finds that 'even when Montaigne thinks (or we think) it has been set aside, [reading] infiltrates everything he writes' (133), and importantly, 'it is a mistake to make too sharp a distinction between the explicit and the implicit, or between theory and practice' (134).[4] The character of his discourse is clearly evident in Montaigne's 'Of repentance',[5] an essay Woolf alludes to in her *Common Reader* essay, 'Montaigne', to be discussed later in this chapter. Here he describes his world and how he has chosen to interact with it:

> The world is but perennial movement. All things in it are in constant motion . . . I cannot keep my subject still. . . . I do not portray his being: I portray passing. Not the passing from one age to another . . . but from day to day, from minute to minute. . . . If my mind could gain a firm footing, I would not make essays, I would make decisions; but it is always in apprenticeship and on trial. (III:2, 610–11)

His mind, not on 'firm footing' and clearly on trial, is, in itself, 'essayistic'. Given my decision to ground this study in the 'essayistic' writings of Montaigne, it is most appropriate to begin with his creation, the 'essay', and Woolf's early connection with Montaigne's *Essays*.

In 1903, on the occasion of her twenty-first birthday, Virginia Woolf wrote to thank her brother Thoby for his gift of a translation of Montaigne's essays.[6] She notes that she was 'getting quite desperate', had 'hunted him 3 years', and 'always read Montaigne in bed' (*LI* 66). Exploring Woolf's lifelong relationship with Montaigne's *Essays* – and, one could say, with 'Montaigne' as he is constructed by Michel de Montaigne – one finds two writers writing about the complex processes of writing and reading. Obviously, her early relationship with the sixteenth-century writer who gave his creation, the 'essay', its significantly indeterminate name began quite early, and as we know from her writings, lasted a lifetime. Over this period, Woolf's letters, diary, essays and reading notes have made reference to Montaigne, his writings and his world view, indicating a deep respect for his talent, his ideas and his humanity. In one of her earliest essays on the 'essay', 'The Decay of Essay-Writing' (1905), her narrator alludes to problems with traditional forms of expression. Utilising a metaphor of ever-changing fashions to refer to the various forms writing might take, Woolf, with her awareness of the market, finds that there are an 'infinite variety of fashions in the external shapes of our wares', and a definite need to stir the 'stale palate' of the British public by giving 'fresh and amusing shapes to the old commodities' – those 'old commodities' representing the culturally constructed genres available to Woolf at that time. And so, at that very early stage of her writing career, she calls for new modes of expression, and with characteristic equivocation, she asserts: 'Perhaps the most significant of these literary inventions is the invention of the personal essay.' She points out that it is at least as old as Montaigne, 'but we count him the first of the moderns' (*EI* 25).

Woolf's writing about her own writing in an early journal entry during her visit to Florence in 1909 – while working on *The Voyage Out* – is quite revealing. Now a critic of her own writing – she deems her own 'descriptive writing' 'too definite', and declares this both 'dangerous & tempting' – she already has the insight at this early stage to know that 'what one records is really the state of one's own mind' (*PA* 395–6). At this time, she had been reading Montaigne for about ten years, and was likely to be familiar with his many references to his mind's connection to his style. For Montaigne, 'the open form of the *Essais* resembles a stroll ... for the thinking itself is taking a stroll' (I:50, 219). Thus we find the agreement expressed in his well-known sentence: 'My style and my mind alike go roaming' (III:9, 761).

Later, in 'A Book of Essays' (1918), she speaks of the risks of essay-writing, stating that 'it is no more than a dance upon a tight rope, where if a single caper is cut clumsily the acrobat suffers death or humiliation before our eyes.' Obviously, a journey such as the essay's – with its unknown destination – is filled with a certain degree of anxiety. On the other hand, she speaks of 'the most delightful parts of Montaigne's essays' and points to 'those where he breaks from the consideration of some abstract quality to explore the peculiarities of his body or his soul'. Unlike many essayists Woolf finds somewhat inadequate to the task, she is quite pleased that Montaigne does not have 'the least fear of giving himself away' (*EI* 212, 214).

Woolf's admiration for Montaigne as an essayist is also expressed in 'The Elizabethan Lumber Room' (1925), where she compares Elizabethan prose and French prose, in this case using Montaigne's *Essays* and Philip Sidney's *Defense of Poesie*. Comparing passages, she finds Sidney's prose 'an uninterrupted monologue, with sudden flashes of felicity and splendid phrases ... but it is never quick, never colloquial, unable to grasp a thought closely and firmly, or to adapt itself flexibly and exactly to the chops and changes of the mind.' In Montaigne, she finds 'a master of an instrument which knows its own powers and limitations, and is capable of insinuating itself into crannies and crevices which poetry can never reach'. For Woolf, 'an age seems to separate Sidney from Montaigne,' and 'the English compared with the French are as boys compared with men' (*CRI* 44).

She also refers to Montaigne in other essays, and notes that Laurence Sterne, another writer venerated by Woolf, also loved Montaigne. She links Sterne with Montaigne in her comment about *Tristram Shandy*: 'The form of the book, which seems to allow the writer to put down at once the first thought that comes into his head, suggests freedom' (*EI* 284). The ability to 'say whatever comes into one's head' is something she appropriates from Montaigne, and finds the courage of this act quite admirable. In her essay about Sterne's *A Sentimental Journey*, the 'usual ceremonies and conventions which keep reader and writer at arm's length disappear. We are as close to life as we can be' (*CRII* 79). The allusions to constraining 'ceremonies and conventions', the closeness of the reader/writer relationship, and most importantly, the closeness to 'life', is frequently appropriated from the writings of Montaigne, as Woolf continues to express her admiration for his writings.

She found many of his memorable expressions written on the beams of his famous Tower in the Dordogne region of France. She and Leonard visited Montaigne's Tower, the site of his writings, for the first time in 1931, and returned in 1937 and 1938. There, she examined 'the fifty-seven "sentences" he had painted on the rafters of his library ceiling'.[7] Exhilarated by her presence in his library, she wrote six letters in two days, to Vita Sackville-West, Vanessa Bell and Ethel Smyth. Writing to Ethel, she related her drunken state, 'drinking a whole bottle of Montizillac, eating paté de foie gras', and being absolutely enthralled to be in the place where the *Essays* were created (317). And to Vita:

> Yesterday was the best of all. We went to Montaigne – a hill in the middle of vineyards, where the Tower still stands; and the very door, room, stairs, and windows where, in which – grammar gone – Montaigne wrote his essays: also his saddle and a view precisely the same he saw. Does this excite you? (*LIV* 318)

On the same day Woolf also wrote about this visit in a letter to her sister, Vanessa, stating that Montaigne's house was 'immensely excit- ing', but in writing to Ethel Smyth once again, her rapture returned, as it had done with Vita: 'My word, Ethel, the very door he opened is there: the steps, worn into deep waves, up to the tower: the 3 windows; writing table, chair, view, vine, dogs, everything precisely as it was' (*LIV* 318, 319, 321). Well, perhaps not the dogs!

Her 1931 diary also shows Montaigne's impact on her other works, in this case an idea for an early draft of *Three Guineas*: 'I read Montaigne this morning & found a passage about the passions of women – their voracity – which I at once opposed to Squire's remarks & so made up a whole chapter of my Tap at the Door' (*DIV* 42). Woolf is referring to passages from Montaigne's 'On Some Verses of Virgil' that are pertinent to her subject:

> In our author's opinion we treat them inconsiderately in the following way. We have discovered, he says, that they [women] are incomparably more capable and ardent than we in the acts of love . . .; but she actually in one night was good for twenty-five encounters, changing company according to her need and liking,

> Her secret parts burning and tense with lust,
> And tired by men, but far from sated, she withdrew.
>
> Juvenal (III:5, 649–50)

There is more in this essay relating to the passions of women, but more pertinent perhaps to *Three Guineas* is the following:

> Women are not wrong at all when they reject the rules of life that have been introduced into the world, inasmuch as it is the men who have made these without them. (III:5, 649)

This essay, with regard to significant gender issues in Montaigne, is also referred to in the Fifth Essay of Woolf's *The Pargiters*; here Montaigne is pitted against Tennyson, where Montaigne 'held that the passion of a woman was by nature stronger than that of a man; but was repressed, very painfully, by the rigours of convention. Tennyson, on the other hand . . . held that women's passions were intrinsically weaker than those of his sex' (109–10). Julia Watson also notes that 'Montaigne differs from his contemporaries in the numerous discourses through which reflections on gender circulate in the *Essais* – masculinity, the body and the senses, the destabilising of oppositions' (Watson 125). The problematics of gender and identity are also integral to the nature of the 'essayistic', as well as the difficulties in exploring its generic placement. Watson also notes Simone de Beauvoir's assessment of Montaigne's stance: 'Montaigne both speaks from within a system of fixed gender relations in the 16th century that is patriarchal and hierarchical and critiques the binary opposition of gender arrangements by which women become the other' (123).[8] The 'essay', defined by its indefiniteness, is, like woman, also deemed 'other', 'outside' and resistant to definition.

In a similar way, as we investigate the problematics of genre, we will begin in sixteenth-century France, with the varied definitions of the 'essay'. Reflecting Montaigne's original designation of his *essai* as 'an attempt', it also establishes the essayistic mode as an activity – as 'the action or process of trying or testing' – and also, 'a trial specimen', 'a taste' or 'a rough copy'. It may also be construed as a 'risk', and given its etymology, according to Philippe Desan, the word 'refers directly to *exagium*, . . . to balance and to weighing, for Montaigne is engaged in a veritable weighing of the most diverse events'. In his readings of his favorite authors – Plato and Socrates, for 'dialogue'; Seneca, 'chosen for his open and easy style; and Plutarch, for 'his taste for psychological portraits' – Desan notes in works of this period 'a horizontal richness that can only be expressed in a contradictory and piecemeal fashion, rather than a vertical hierarchy' (Friedrich xx, xviii, xix).[9]

The contradictory, so evident in the writings of Woolf and Montaigne, is also an important quality for the 'essayistic', as it reflects its resistance to singularity, to fixity, to the limitations of generic labels, as well as its need for the clash of oppositional voices. In speaking about genre, Thomas Kent notes its less than monolithic state: 'In one sense, a genre is a system of codifiable conventions, and in another sense, it is a continually changing cultural artifact' (Kent 15). But given this assessment, a set of readers still must agree, at an historical moment, that a particular configuration of words can be construed under a certain title, and the marginalised in most cultures do not make these decisions. W. Wolfgang Holdheim, on the other hand, refers to Montaigne's 'essay' as 'an antigenre, designed to flaunt the prescriptiveness in literary matters which had been inherited from a rationalistic tradition' (Holdheim 20). Georg Lukács, in his 1911 collection of essays, *Soul and Form*, identifies the essay with criticism; in this pre-Marxist phase, Lukács viewed the essay as 'a judgment, but the essential, the value-determining thing about it is not the verdict (as in the case with the system) but the process of judging' (Lukács 17–18). Both Walter Benjamin and Theodor Adorno also accept the essay as a critique of systems, and in 'The Essay as Form', Adorno presents his theory of the essay as critique: 'The essay rejects the identity principle upon which all systems are based. . . . It also refuses the ontological priorities of systems – their privileging of the timeless over the historical, the universal over the particular' (158) and finds that the essay's innermost formal law is heresy (171). According to Adorno, the essay is structured 'in such a way that it could always, at any point, break off. It thinks in fragments just as reality is fragmented, and gains [its] unity by moving through fissures, rather than by smoothing them over' (161). The essay, utilised as ideological critique, is always in process, and attempts to harness it will always fail.

According to Hugo Friedrich, the dialogue and letter are part of the prehistory of Montaigne's open-form language, with the letter always referred to as 'half of a dialogue'. Montaigne liked the Platonic dialogue, and also the scepticism of Plato, for in his view 'the dialogue is the writer's actualization of the withholding of judgment, the impossibility of fixing in place either the spirit or the subjects . . . and can depict its wealth and changing perspectives by distributing material among several persons' (Friedrich 360). This strategy for the inclusion of other voices is evident in the numbers of quotations in Montaigne's *Essays*; according to Thomas Recchio's Bakhtinian reading, Montaigne's essay is 'an exploration of his experience of language as much as an explanation of his experience of the world and his shifting sense of self as it is created and transformed through writing' (Recchio 281). This dialogic aspect of the Montaignean essay, its inclusion of many other voices, creates a situation not unlike our everyday discourse with others; we are, after all, constantly interpreting speech, conversation, actions and our own expectations, as Bakhtin so aptly suggests:

> We can go so far as to say that in real life people talk most of all about what others talk about – they transmit, recall, weigh, and pass judgment on other people's words, opinions, assertions, information . . . At every step one meets a 'quotation' or a 'reference' to something that a particular person said . . . to one's own previous words, to a newspaper . . . Thus talk goes on about speaking people and their words everywhere. (*DI* 338–9)

The problematic nature of these activities – interpreting and quoting other voices – was also conveyed by Montaigne to his readers in the 1580s:

> It is more of a job to interpret the interpretations than to interpret the things, and there are more books about books than about any other subject: we do nothing but write glosses about each other. The world is swarming with commentaries: of authors there is a great scarcity. (III:13, 818)

Woolf and Montaigne, in their many acts of interpretation, struggle with other voices – as their readers struggle – to make language their own, to find their own multiple voices, and to form their own opinions; no unitary voice of certainty prevails. And so these voices, quotations and conversations, incorporated into essayistic texts, enable a struggle with those varied voices within the text – as well as those voices that populate the minds of different readers. M. M. Bakhtin writes of this struggle:

> The importance of struggling with another's discourse, its influence in the history of an individual's coming to ideological consciousness, is enormous. One's own discourse and one's own voice, although born of another or dynamically stimulated by another, will sooner or later begin to liberate themselves from the authority of the other's discourse. (*DI* 348)

In speaking of struggling with opposing voices, of contradiction of his opinions, Montaigne finds that 'they neither offend nor affect me; they merely arouse and exercise me,' for 'when someone opposes me, he arouses my attention, not my anger. I go to meet a man who contradicts me, who instructs me' (III:8, 705).

It is important to note the many links between Montaigne, Bakhtin and Woolf, in their assessments of the multifaceted nature of words, the 'life' of words, and especially their descriptions of a reading process that has links with reader-response theories.[10] Although no one has made any direct link between Bakhtin and Montaigne's writings, Bakhtin's dissertation on Rabelais, one of Montaigne's contemporaries, entitled

Rabelais and His World,[11] quotes several of Montaigne's essays, and my examination of their ideas regarding the relationship between reader and writer is quite illuminating (emphasis added):

> Speech belongs *half to the speaker, half to the listener*. The latter must prepare to receive it according to the motion it takes. As among tennis players, the receiver moves and makes ready according to the motion of the striker and the nature of the stroke.
>
> Montaigne (III:13, 834; 3, 13)

> As a living, socio-ideological concrete thing, as heteroglot opinion, *language*, for the individual consciousness, *lies on the borderline between oneself and the other. The word in language is half someone else's*. It becomes 'one's own' only when the speaker populates it with his own intention, his own accent, when he appropriates the word, adapting it to his own semantic and expressive intention. Prior to this moment of appropriation, the word does not exist in a neutral and impersonal language (it is not, after all, out of a dictionary that the speaker gets his words!), but rather it exists in other people's mouths, in other people's contexts, serving other people's intentions.
>
> M. M. Bakhtin (*DI* 291)

> The first process, to receive impressions with the utmost understanding, is *only half the process of reading*; it must be completed, if we are to get the whole pleasure from a book, by another. We must pass judgment upon these multitudinous impressions; we must make of these fleeting shapes one that is hard and lasting.
>
> Woolf, 'How Should One Read A Book?' (*CRII* 266)

Their focus on the shared quality of this relationship – that the word 'half' is part of all three excerpts of their writings on this topic – suggests the significance of the interaction, with the Montaigne's 'half' suggesting the dependency on the tennis court, each side 'reading' the move of the other and positioning themselves accordingly. Bakhtin speaks of 'the borderline between oneself and the other', with the word in language being 'half someone else's' (*DI* 293–4), while Woolf finds that 'the first process, to receive impressions with the utmost understanding, is only half the process of reading; it must be completed, if we are to get the whole pleasure from a book, by another' (*CRII* 266–7). They all share the dialogic aspect on this complicated process. My continued reading of Bakhtin's quotation, however, leads us back to Woolf's commentary on language in her essay/broadcast, 'Craftsmanship'.

Comparison of the last part of my quotation from Bakhtin with Woolf's commentary on language from 'Craftsmanship' certainly gives one pause. Although Woolf and Bakhtin were writing during similar periods – 1920s, 1930s and 1940 – there is no evidence that they knew of each other's writings, but it is always interesting to stumble upon such similarity, even in translation from Russian.

From Bakhtin's last sentence, his parenthetical statement relating to dictionaries, together with what follows, could easily have emerged from Woolf's 'Craftsmanship'. Here Bakhtin states that '(it is not, after all, out of a dictionary that the speaker gets his words!), but rather it exists in other people's mouths, in other people's contexts, serving other people's intentions' (Bakhtin, *DI* 293–4). Woolf's narrator in 'Craftsmanship' relates that 'words do not live in dictionaries; they live in the mind' (*DM* 204), and she also finds that words 'have been out and about, on people's lips, in their houses, in the streets, in the fields, for so many centuries' (203). As noted above, Montaigne informed his readers as to the whereabouts of words and their transformational abilities: 'I do not portray being; I portray passing' (III:2, 601–11). 'My conceptions and my judgment', he wrote, 'move only by groping, staggering, stumbling, and blundering' and so 'I let my thoughts run on' (I:27, 107). 'My understanding does not always go forward, it goes backward too' in 'a drunkard's motion, staggering, dizzy, wobbling, or that of reeds that the wind stirs haphazardly as it pleases' (III:9, 736).

Perhaps one of the most important questions regarding the problems of definition of the 'essayistic' belongs to Richard L. Regosin: 'We are still (or perhaps, always) concerned with lexical problems, with questions of definition: What is this "life" that is being written in the *Essays*?' and he finds that 'the writing itself is the very process of formation; it is its life' (Regosin 99, 100). For him,

> we find [Montaigne] not only in his personal references and anecdotes but in his rhetorical figures, not only in his opinions about friendship or about education but in his syntactical structures, not only in his quotations and classical allusions but in the semantic richness of his lexicon and its patterns of repetition, association, and opposition. (Regosin 100)

We also find Virginia Woolf in these places, and this takes us to Toril Moi's oft-quoted comments regarding Woolf's textual practice. We do find, in Montaigne and Woolf, multiple links between their aesthetics and their politics, and looking back to Moi's Kristevan approach to Woolf, many agree with her view of 'locating the politics of Woolf's writing precisely in her textual practice' (Moi 16). That Moi utilises one of Woolf's favorite words – 'precisely', which Woolf generally uses to undermine some reference to certainty – is quite interesting here. Although I agree with Moi's assessment, I would also want to complicate it by noting Rita Felski's concerns regarding a strict 'equivalence' between 'experimentalism and oppositionality', for, according to Felski, this equation 'fails to theorize the contingent functions of textual forms in relation to socially differentiated publics at particular historical moments' or 'the changing social meanings of textual forms' (Felski 161). Felski also suggests that 'radical impulses are not inherent in the formal properties of texts; they can be realized only through interactions between texts and readers' (161). Here I would note that both Montaigne and Woolf – in their 'essayistic' mode of expression – foreground the interactions between reader and text, as well as the contingent functions of their textual practice, including the complex interaction between the minds and bodies of those involved.

How does one make judgements about books? What happens to the mind/body when one reads? What transformations potentially take place? What are the risks of arranging words on a page, never to be changed, of exposing one's inner self, taking a stand, risking the uncertainty of acceptance by readers, risking rebellion, protest or perhaps submission, all the while encumbered by the traditions and conventions that have held sway for generations? And how is all of the above inflected by language, gender, genre, culture, period, nation, religion, and the multitude of environmental factors too numerous to mention? And how, as Woolf's narrator directs the reader in 'How Should One Read a Book?', do you 'make [your] own experiment with the dangers and difficulties of words' and gain the courage to 'come to your own conclusions' (258–9) and, perhaps, state them out loud. Maybe deciding how to value written or spoken language is most difficult, for 'there is always the demon in us who whispers, "I hate, I love," and we cannot silence him. Indeed, it is precisely because we hate and we love that our relation with the poets is so intimate' (268). As Kate Flint suggests: 'In Woolf's descriptions of reading experiences, the cerebral frequently mingles with the tactile, the febrile, even the fetishistic: a combination of pleasures which, she suggests, surpass sexual activity itself.' As reflected in Woolf's 'Phases of Fiction', 'the novels which make us live imaginatively' involve 'the whole of the body as well as the mind' (189).[12]

Montaigne, composing his *Essays* in the 1580s, also finds that text, body and mind are inseparable, and 'promotes an anatomical discourse in which a metaphorical equivalence is established between text and body', so 'the figures of Montaigne's discourse represent erotic codings revealing traces of concealed desire' (Kritzman 81–2).[13] Feelings permeate Montaigne's writings, and given his scepticism regarding the laws and conventions of the late Renaissance, he writes that he might 'negligently let myself be guided by the general law of the world'; yet he always questions these imposed rules. Importantly, his judgements will be his own: 'I shall know it well enough when I feel it' (III:13, 821). Woolf's narrator similarly underscores the dangers of succumbing to 'authorities', 'laws' and 'conventions', in 'How Should One Read a Book?': 'our taste, the nerve of sensation that send shocks through us, is our chief illuminant; we learn through feeling' (*CRII* 268).

And in Woolf's 1920 essay, 'Pure English', a review of *Gammer Gurton's Needle*, a 1575 work contemporaneous with Montaigne, 'the ordinary reader' acknowledges that 'it is his feeling, and not the reasons for his feeling, that is of interest,' for 'an irrational element enters into their liking and disliking for books as certainly as it enters their feelings for people' (*EIII* 235). In the relationship between the reader and the book, 'the essence of it is instinctive rather than rational':

> It is personal, complex, as much composed of the reader's temperament perhaps as of the writer's. To make a clean breast of it, hour and season and mood, the day's brightness or the moment's despondency, all weigh down the scales. With such impressionable instruments are we provided; of such unstable elements are our judgments compounded. No wonder that a second reading often reverses the verdict of the first. (*EIII* 236)

Woolf's multifaceted concept of the 'personal' can be found parcelled out in many of her essays – each referring to a specific essayist, and each giving us yet another aspect of what this term means to her. In her essay, 'Reading' (1919), Woolf alludes to the works of Sir Thomas Browne, one of the first of the essayists to be 'definitely himself' (155). Here, he gives his readers the gift of 'the more splendid picture of his soul to feast upon. In that dark world, he was one of the explorers' (155). In short, Woolf tells us: 'Sir Thomas Browne brings in the whole question, which is afterwards to become of such importance, of knowing one's author. Somewhere, everywhere, now hidden, now apparent in whatever is written down is the form of a human being' (156). And about William Hazlitt, Woolf writes: 'His essays are emphatically himself. He has no reticence and he has no shame' (*CRII* 173). A few years later, in 'The Modern Essay' (1922), Woolf seems disappointed that 'this sense of intimacy' (222), present in the essay since Montaigne, was last found in the essays of Charles Lamb. In Max Beerbohm, however, she relates that, some time in the 1890s, readers found themselves 'addressed by a voice which seemed to belong to a man no larger than themselves' (217). This lack of hierarchy between the voice of the essayist and the reader addressed will become a crucial aspect of Woolf's essayistic mode. Here Woolf also finds an essayist 'capable of using the essayists' most proper but most dangerous and delicate tool', for Max Beerbohm

> has brought personality into literature, not unconsciously and impurely, but so consciously and purely that we do not know whether there is any relation between Max the essayist and Mr. Beerbohm the man. We only know that the spirit of personality permeates every word that he writes. (222)

But that 'self' to which Woolf alludes in 'The Modern Essay' is viewed quite problematically by Woolf, for while she considers the self 'essential to literature, it is also its most dangerous antagonist'. It is also the paradox: '*Never to be yourself and yet always – that is the problem*' (217; emphasis mine). Jane Gallop, in *The Daughter's Seduction*, seems to resolve the problem of women's resistance to being essentialised, but also her desire for identity as a woman. She suggests that, 'Identity must be continually assumed, and immediately called into question' (Gallop xii).[14] Carl H. Klaus,[15] in his fascinating reading and re-reading of 'The Modern Essay', finds this paradoxical conception of the essayist's persona 'both an authentic reflection and a fictionalized construction of personality' (Klaus 32). In his essay on Woolf's essay, he looks back over his thirty-seven-year relationship with this particular piece, over a period which includes multiple readings, each interrupted by a varying number of years away from it. Here he communicates to his own readers his continuing desire 'to meet it ['The Modern Essay'] again and again', and also his 'finding it altered upon each visit'. In the process he enacts the narrator's own response to an effective essay, and also admits to 'finding [himself] altered each time as well' (Klaus 33). Here he also relates his failure, after so many readings, 'to notice that arresting metaphor in which she conceives of reading a good essay as comparable to carrying on a highly civilized acquaintance or friendship with someone' (Klaus 33). For Woolf, those books she encounters in a book-case are very much alive:

> You have not finished with it because you have read it, any more than friendship is ended because it is time to part. Life wells up and alters and adds. Even things in a book-case change if they are alive; we find ourselves waiting to meet them again and again; we find them altered. (*CR1* 222)

This sense of 'life' plays a crucial part of her 1924 essay, 'Indiscretions', in which 'reading' is compared with 'liking and disliking' and with 'our whole day stained and steeped by the affections'. And although 'the critic may be able to abstract the essence and feast upon it undisturbed, for the rest of us in every book there is something – sex, character, temperament – which, *as in life*, rouses affection or repulsion, and, *as in life*, sways and prejudices; and again, *as in life*, is hardly to be analyzed by reason' (*EIII* 460; emphasis added).

Life and death, in all their metaphoric splendour, pervade the writings of Woolf and Montaigne, and Woolf frequently – and self-consciously – appropriates Montaigne's varying references to 'life'. In her essay, 'Montaigne', written for her *Common Reader*, Woolf appropriates fifteen of Montaigne's 107 essays; her selection, of course, 'reads [her]', as we are told in 'Notes on an Elizabethan Play' (*CRI* 48). In the process of exploring Woolf's interest in the 'life' Montaigne expresses with his essays, I will also focus on several of her chosen essays, for they clearly reveal her significant concerns. It is not surprising that her narrator begins by expressing how difficult it is 'to tell the truth about oneself', and provides the reader with Montaigne's words: 'tis a rugged road, more so than it seems, to follow a pace so rambling and uncertain, as that of the soul' (*CRI* 59, 'Of Exercitation').

> The pen [the reader is told] is a rigid instrument; it can say very little; it has all kinds of habits and ceremonies of its own. It is dictatorial too: it is always making ordinary men into prophets, and changing the natural stumbling trip of human speech into the solemn and stately march of pens. It is for this reason that Montaigne stands out from the legions of the dead with such irrepressible vivacity. (59)

With its military imagery of the deadness, the rigidity of 'marching pens', Montaigne's book was his 'life'. Moving to politics, Woolf's narrator notes that 'statesmen are always praising the greatness of Empire, and preaching the moral duty of civilising the savage.' Here Montaigne speaks 'in a burst of rage': '"So many cities levelled with the ground, so many nations exterminated . . . and the richest and most beautiful part of the world turned upside down for the traffic of pearl and pepper! Mechanic victories!"' (*CRI* 60, 'Of Coaches'). Montaigne's essay on colonialism, explored in more detail in Chapter 4, certainly influenced Woolf's views, as one expects. Continuing to refer to the 'soul', 'the life within', the narrator provides an enlightening description:

> Really she is the strangest creature in the world, far from heroic, variable as a weathercock, 'bashful, insolent; chaste, lustful; prating, silent; laborious, delicate; ingenious, heavy; melancholic, pleasant; lying, true; knowing, ignorant; liberal, covetous, and prodigal' – in short, so complex, so indefinite, corresponding so little to the version which does duty for her in public, that a man might spend his life merely trying to run her to earth. (*CRI* 60)

These oppositions are a pervasive part of Montaigne's strategy; in this case, an overload to make the point. As the reader is told: 'Once conform, once do what other people do because they do it, and a lethargy steals over all the finer nerves and faculties of the soul. She becomes all outer show and inward emptiness; dull, callous, and indifferent' (61). The narrator had just explained the positive qualities of 'the man who is aware of himself', the man who 'lives', for he is 'independent' and 'never bored'. Assuming an explanation from Montaigne – as 'this master of the art of life' – the narrator finds that 'he is by no means explicit.' Receiving 'no plain answers' from that 'subtle half smiling, half melancholy man', she learns of the need to 'observe oneself'. Desiring that Montaigne enlighten us more precisely, he only states that 'one must not lay down rules,' for we must allow souls to have 'free play' (62). And the words that permeate the text – 'for', 'but', 'perhaps' and 'if' – come right from Montaigne's essay, 'Of Cripples', where he also adds 'It seems to me' and states: 'It makes me hate probable things when they are planted on me as infallible. I like the words which soften and moderate the rashness of our propositions' (III:11, 788). Woolf places it in her essay slightly changed: '"Perhaps" is one of his favourite expressions; "perhaps" and "I think" and all those words which qualify the rash assumptions of human ignorance. Such words help one to muffle up opinions which it would be highly impolitic to speak outright' (63). And his ideas regarding the referentiality of language, in another essay included in Woolf's essay, 'Montaigne', also echo her thinking: 'Ceremony forbids our expressing in words things that are permissible and natural, and we obey it; reason forbids our doing things that are illicit and wicked, and no one obeys it' (II:17, 479).

In reading Montaigne's view that 'we respect those who sacrifice themselves in public service, load them with honours, and pity them for allowing, as they must, the inevitable compromise' (63), many of us think of our current leaders and other members of our governments, but to no avail. For Montaigne (and Woolf), 'movement and change are the essence of our being; rigidity is death; conformity is death: let us say what comes into our heads, repeat ourselves, contradict ourselves, fling out the wildest nonsense . . . for nothing matters except life; and, of course, order' (63). The abruptness of this change – the move from 'freedom' and 'change' to 'order' – is repeated in her essays, 'On Not Knowing Greek', 'The Modern Essay' and 'Modern Fiction'. The monitor, 'an invisible censor within' is 'the judge to whom we must submit' so we may 'achieve that order' (63). Despite these contradictory and qualifying words, there is something which seems definitive: 'These essays are an attempt to communicate a soul.' Noted as 'truth', 'health' and 'happiness', communication is expressed and enacted by Montaigne's essays. This, of course, given his stature during Woolf's lifetime, makes these statements somewhat ironic. But she ends the essay with increasing repetition, reiterating the freedom to 'say the first thing that comes into our heads', and that 'it is life that matters,' 'it is life that emerges, more and more clearly as these essays reach not their end but their suspension in full career' (66). And then, going back to the soul, we are asked to 'observe', as this word is used six times in this essay: to 'observe' how the soul is 'always casting her own lights and shadows; makes the substantial hollow and the frail substantial'. And with all that is in opposition, we are advised to 'observe, too, her duplicity, her complexity' – for the soul 'believes, doesn't believe'. 'Observe,' for 'even now in 1580, no one has any clear knowledge – such cowards are we – such lovers of the smooth conventional ways' (67). We are admonished to 'Observe, observe perpetually,' as we hear one final question from 'the master of the art of life', for in his volumes 'we have heard the pulse and rhythm of the soul' for 'here is some one who succeeded in the hazardous enterprise of living.' And 'by means of perpetual experiment' and 'observation', he succeeded in his life. Next come the inevitable questions regarding the 'soul', the desire 'to communicate with others', the 'mystery of life', and, as there are no answers, there is that one question: 'Que scais-je?' It is also Woolf's question, and the question that pervades the world – as we near the end of the first decade of the twenty-first century.

Woolf's essay, 'Modern Fiction', resonates with the questions of 'life' and 'freedom' that also permeated 'Montaigne' and so many of her other writings, for it is the nature of the 'essayistic' to convey movement, action and a certain wildness. As the narrator conveys regarding the desire to write better: 'we do not come to write better; all that we can be said to do is to keep moving, now a little in this direction, now in that, but with a circular tendency' (*CRI* 146). Beginning with the military language of battles, and looking for new modes of writing, readers are confronted with an immediate opposition:

> We *only know* that *certain* gratitudes and hostilities inspire us; that *certain* paths *seem* to lead to *fertile* land, others to the *dust* and the *desert*; and of this *perhaps may* be worth while to *attempt* some account. (146; emphasis added).

I have emphasised the words Woolf uses in this sentence to show – as her narrators show – how the information is being communicated. 'Knowledge' and 'certainty' are opposed to equivocal words like 'seem' and 'perhaps', while the two paths are placed in opposition, expressing the 'life' of 'fertile' land, and the 'dust' and 'desert' of death. Then provisionality is foregrounded with an 'essayistic' 'attempt'. This continues throughout the essay, as the narrators thank Mr. Wells, Mr. Bennett and Mr. Galsworthy for 'what they *might* have done but have not done; what we *certainly* could not do, but as *certainly*, *perhaps*, do not wish to do. No single phrase will sum up the charge or grievance which we have to bring' (147; emphasis added). The equivocation mounts as questions regarding the important aspects of their writings end with the possibility that 'life should refuse to live there?' and 'if we label them', and 'we are exacting – what are we exacting? (we don't explain),' for the narrators tell us: 'we frame our questions differently at different times . . . Is that worth while? What is the point of it all? . . . Mr Bennett has come down with his magnificent apparatus for catching life just an inch or two on the wrong side? Life escapes; and perhaps without life nothing else is worthwhile' (149).

It is significant that the narrators will 'hazard an opinion' about the form of fiction in vogue, about the 'life' or 'spirit', 'truth or reality', for 'this, the essential thing, has moved off, or on, and refuses to be contained in such ill-fitting vestments as we provide' (149). The 'style' and the 'mind' are not in conjunction as they were in Montaigne: 'My style and my mind go roaming' (III:9, 761). Here the tyrant has the writer constrained – 'to provide a plot, to provide comedy, tragedy, love interest' and these genres, conventions and customs have 'an air of probability embalming the whole' (149), and the questions regarding 'life' reappear: 'Is life like this? Must novels be like this?' With the mind receiving 'incessant showers', 'myriad impressions', falling into the opposing categories of either the 'trivial, fantastic, evanescent, or engraved with the sharpness of steel' (150), contradictions abound, as questions regarding 'the proper stuff of fiction' appear. We know from Montaigne that everything is the 'proper stuff of fiction', as Woolf invokes 'the Rheumatism of the left shoulder' in 'How Should One Read a Book?' and in *A Room of One's Own*. For Montaigne, 'A fly will serve my purpose. Any topic is equally fertile for me' (III:5, 668). That 'life exists in all things' (*CRI* 151), that 'any method is right,' and the courage to choose not 'this' but 'that' is invoked in the freedom to 'set down what he chooses' (152). The impossibility to say that 'this is comic' or 'this is tragic,' or that 'short stories' should be 'conclusive', reflects the 'essayistic', the resistance to genre, to constraints, to a lack of freedom 'to say what comes into our heads'.

Finally, 'it is the sense that there is no answer,' for life goes on and on 'with question after question which must be left to sound on and on . . . in hopeless interrogation that fills us with a deep, and finally it may be with a resentful, despair. But perhaps, we see something that escapes them' – like life – 'or why should the voice of protest mix with our gloom? The voice of protest . . . seems to have bred in us the instinct to enjoy and fight rather than to suffer and understand' (*CRI* 153–4). The active, the participatory, is opposed to passive complacency, with the body inseparable from the mind, and I would concur with Jane Goldman's finding that 'critical focus on the "luminous halo" passage has meant a lack of attention to the oppositional energies at work in "Modern Fiction"' (Goldman 70). The oppositional discourse is present as one examines the contradictory language, the active, participatory versus the passive complacency. That 'there is no limit to the horizon,' and that 'no method, no experiment, even the wildest – is forbidden, but only falsity and pretence' also harkens back to Montaigne. And in imagining the 'art of fiction come alive and standing in our midst, she would undoubtedly bid us break her and bully her, as well as honour and love her' (154), for these contradictions bring 'renewal' and 'sovereignty'. Nothing could better express the contradictions so pervasive in the writings of Montaigne and Woolf, which give new life to these writings and permeate the very words that they use. Ralph Waldo Emerson, in writing about Montaigne's *Essays*, said of the French writer's words: 'cut these words and they will bleed; they are vascular and alive' (Emerson 102).[16] These are the words Virginia Woolf describes in 'Craftsmanship', for they too are alive.

Notes

1. Harold Brodkey (1985), 'Reading is the Most Dangerous Game', *New York Times Book Review* (24 Nov.), 44. Quoted in John A. McCarthy's excellent study (1989), *Crossing Boundaries: History and Theory of Essay-Writing in Germany, 1690–1815*, Philadelphia, PA: University of Pennsylvania Press.
2. See essay (1950), 'Leslie Stephen', *The Captain's Death Bed*, New York, NY: Harcourt Brace Jovanovich, 62–75. Stephen, Virginia Woolf's father, was editor of the *Dictionary of National Biography* (1885–91) and of *Cornhill Magazine* (1871), and wrote *Hours in the Library* (1874, 1879) and *The Science of Ethics* (1882). He gave the fifteen-year-old Virginia Stephen access to his well-stocked library and purchased many books specifically for her.
3. R. Lane Kauffmann (1989), 'The Skewed Path: Essaying as Unmethodical Method', in *Essays on the Essay*, ed. Alexander J. Butrym, Athens, GA: University of Georgia Press.
4. See Terence Cave (1987), 'Problems of Reading in the *Essais*', in *Michel de Montaigne*, ed. Harold Bloom, New York, NY: Chelsea.
5. Michel de Montaigne (1965), *The Complete Essays of Montaigne*, trans. Donald M. Frame, Stanford, CA: Stanford University Press. All subsequent quotations are from this edition.
6. For her birthday, her brother Thoby found Virginia Woolf an English translation of Montaigne's *Essays* from 1685, translated by Cotton; she had been searching for this for three years.
7. Terence Cave points out that there are 1,300 quotations proper (excluding translated or paraphrased passages) in Montaigne's *Essays* (Cave 144).
8. See Julia Watson (1994), 'En-gendering the Essays', in *Approaches to Teaching Montaigne's Essays*. Watson makes reference to Simone de Beauvoir's *The Second Sex*, regarding de Beauvoir's quotations from Montaigne's *Essays* and their focus on gender (50).

9. Philippe Desan edited and introduced *Montaigne*, by Hugo Friedrich (1991), trans. Dawn Eng, Berkeley, CA: University of California Press.

10. See Jane P. Tompkins (1980), *Reader-Response Criticism: From Formalism to Post-Structuralism*, Baltimore, MD: Johns Hopkins University Press.

11. M. M Bakhtin's dissertation, 'Rabelais and Folk Culture of the Middle Ages and the Renaissance', was written in 1940, submitted during WWII and not defended immediately. It was published in 1965 as *Rabelais and his World*, with a later edition (1993) translated by Hélène Iswolsky and published by Indiana University Press, Bloomington. It includes his work on the 'carnivalesque' and 'grotesque realism', and makes references to Montaigne's *Essays*.

12. Kate Flint (1996), 'Reading Uncommonly: Virginia Woolf and the Practice of Reading', *The Yearbook of English Studies* 26, 187–98.

13. Lawrence D. Kritzman (1991), *The Rhetoric of Sexuality and the Literature of the French Renaissance*, Cambridge: Cambridge University Press.

14. Jane Gallop (1982), *The Daughter's Seduction*, Ithaca, NY: Cornell University Press.

15. Carl H. Klaus (1990), 'On Virginia Woolf and the Essay', *Iowa Review* 20(2) (Spring/Summer), 28–34.

16. See Ralph Waldo Emerson (1850), 'Montaigne; or, the Skeptic', in *Representative Men*, London: Routledge, 102.

Chapter 2

Changing Titles/Transforming Texts?

The words hang like a collar round my neck. It is not only that to write of women & fiction would require many many volumes; one can see, even from a distance, that the subject is dangerous.

Virginia Woolf, 'Women & Fiction', *The Manuscript Versions of A Room of One's Own*[1]

It is the words of the title, 'Women & Fiction', that constrain Virginia Woolf's narrator, and it is these words, not surprisingly, that must be 'slipped from [her] neck' if she is to continue writing. But for the narrator, 'the need of coming to some conclusion, on a subject that indeed admits of none, bent [her] head to the ground' (4). When this passage appears in *A Room of One's Own*, it is slightly transformed, for the need to come to a conclusion 'on a subject that raises all sorts of prejudices and passions, bowed [her] head to the ground' (*AROO* 5); it is this aspect – 'all sorts of prejudices and the passions' – perhaps, that called forth the dangers of this subject.

Along with her talks at Newnham and Girton, and her essay, 'Women & Fiction', these manuscript versions make up another of Woolf's four attempts to address this subject.[2] The essay version, written for *Forum* in March 1929, has a very different response to the words of its title:

The title of this article can be read in two ways: it may allude to women and the fiction that they write, or to women and the fiction that is written about them. The ambiguity is intentional, for in dealing with women as writers, as much elasticity as possible is desirable; it is necessary to leave oneself room to deal with other things besides their work, so much has that work been influenced by conditions that have nothing whatever to do with art. (*EV* 28)

Looking back and seeing that 'the history of England is the history of the male line, not of the female,' provides her with a history of 'strange intermissions of silence and speech' (28–9). It is only at the end of this essay – after an assessment that begins with Sappho and Lady Murisaki, and ends with the Victorians, with Brontë and Eliot – that we come to its future title, as her narrator looks ahead to 'leisure, and money, and a room to themselves' (35). But how does this new title, *A Room of One's Own* – now a feminist manifesto – transform its reception? If 'Women & Fiction' is intentionally ambiguous, how does the new title change things? The narrator speaks of 'leaving oneself "room" to deal with other things', and this new title seems less defined, less constraining than 'Women & Fiction', and may offer more space, more trajectories, more suggestiveness for exposing 'the conditions' that have influenced both the women and, concomitantly, their fiction. And since titles are our first contact with a text – along with the jacket design, colours and images – something significant happens with that immediate response, for the words of titles are extremely provocative and, most importantly, titles are imbued with power.

In her 1937 BBC essay/broadcast, Virginia Woolf announced two titles: the title of the series, 'Words Fail Me', and that of her particular talk, 'Craftsmanship'. From this title, the narrator assumes that 'the talker is meant to discuss the craft of words – the craftsmanship of the writer' (*DM* 198). Now, as readers, we are faced with the 'incongruous, unfitting' nature of the term, 'craftsmanship', and told that the English dictionary 'confirms us in our doubts'. Checking the dictionary's definitions for 'craft', the narrator finds two: one refers to the making of useful objects, and the other refers to cajolery, cunning or deceit. Confused by such disparity, she feels certain that 'words never make anything that is useful; and words are the only things that tell the truth and nothing but the truth.' The 'certainty' in the narrator's statements seems clearly unfounded and exaggerated. To bring together these two incongruous ideas, which 'if they mate can only give birth to some monster' (198), is not a viable option. 'Instantly,' we are told, 'the title of the talk must be changed, and for it substituted another – A Ramble round Words, perhaps.' Although designating this her new title – albeit equivocally – Woolf's narrator does not use quotation marks. Perhaps undermining its function as a title, she seems to stress its relevance to the randomness of her essayistic method. Now an essay without its title, an essay referred to as 'a decapitated talk', she compares it to a chicken 'with its head cut off' (*DM* 198). With 'decapitation', the image of Medusa comes to mind, for her potency begins at the point when her head is severed. This, of course, would have been familiar to Woolf from Jane Harrison's work.[3] And so the talk without its originally designated title has, perhaps, a sudden renewal of energy.

This new title, which conveys aimless wandering, is rendered even more tentative by its immediate qualification by 'perhaps'. It suggests circularity – rather than linearity – and clearly denies any constraints on the writer or her language; it also maintains her need for an open, relaxed and indefinite mode of writing. Woolf's 'decapitated talk', a talk without its title, is reminiscent in another context of a discussion on genre by Celeste Schenck. Schenck refers to Marcelin Pleynet[4] in her discussion of a feminist theory of genre in order to emphasise his assessment of the imperialist nature of titles: 'It is indeed the word (novel, poem) placed on the cover of a book which (by convention) programmes or "originates" our reading. We have here (with the genre "novel," "poem") a *masterword* which from the outset reduces complexity, reduces the textual encounter' (Pleynet, quoted by Schenck 284). Clearly, for Woolf, the title 'Craftsmanship', as defined in her dictionary, places too many limitations on her essay; she needs a title open enough to increase the complexity of her text – to expand the textual encounter. Woolf desires a suggestiveness precluded by categories – by dictionary definitions – for 'it is the nature of words to mean many things' (201), and as referenced above: 'words do not live in dictionaries; they live in the mind' (204).

In her desire to prove the uselessness of words, she seeks to show how, 'in forcing them against their nature to be useful . . . we see to our cost how they mislead us, how they fool us' (*DM* 199). Words want us to know that 'it is their nature not to express one simple statement but a thousand possibilities . . . and we are beginning to face the fact.' Giving us 'a language of signs', we are shown the *Michelin Guide* with its 'gables' to designate value; then Baedeker appears with 'stars' (200). But this is not about ratings; this is about the adaptability of this system to 'the whole art of criticism, the whole of literary criticism' and how it could be 'reduced to the size of a sixpenny bit'. Fooling around with this new coded critique, she informs us that 'biographies and novels will be slim and muscular; and a railway company . . . will be fined for improper use of language' (201). And as for 'their power to tell the truth', we are immediately informed that 'according to the dictionary there are at least three kinds of truth: God's or gospel truth; literary truth; and home truth (generally unflattering).' And 'words', we learn, 'if properly used, seem able to live for ever' (201).

Now, we as readers feel that a change is in the offing; we learn that 'a useful statement is a statement that can mean only one thing. And it is the nature of words to mean many things' and some of these will be 'sunken meanings' that suggest many possibilities. The investigation of 'Passing Russell Square', the narrator's example for showing that 'it is the nature of words to mean many things,' focuses attention on the singular 'surface meaning' and 'so many sunken meanings' (201). As the reader is informed:

The word 'passing' suggested the transiency of things, the passage of time and the changes of human life. Then the word 'Russell' suggested the rustling of leaves and the skirt of a polished floor; also the ducal house of Bedford and half the history of England. Finally, the word 'Square' brings in the sight, the shape of an actual square combined with some visual suggestion of the stark angularity of stucco. Thus one sentence of the simplest kind rouses the imagination, the memory, the eye and the ear – all combine in reading it. (*DM* 202)

We are now in the territory of *The Colbert Report*,[5] a US comedy show that frequently takes on the problematics of language in a very comedic mode. For now, in this most focused examination of language, the emphasis shows how words 'combine unconsciously together', as our 'suggestions become unreal', and suddenly, in the following sense, we also 'become unreal – specialists, word mongers, or phrase finders', but clearly 'not readers' (202). It is essential that we remain simply 'readers'. And as readers, 'we have to allow the sunken meanings to remain sunken, suggested, not stated; lapsing and flowing into each other like reeds on the bed of a river.' For we are now in the realm of 'the suggestive power of words', and also in the realm of a very unreliable and extremely witty narrator.

Denying any 'trace of the strange, of the diabolical power which words possess when they are not tapped out by a typewriter but come fresh from the human brain', the narrator asks why then we gain such an image of the writer, his character, his surroundings, and 'how words do this without the writer's will; often against his will' (*DM* 202). But, as is typical of Woolf's essayistic writing, we find that 'this power of suggestion is one of the most mysterious properties of words':

> Words, English words, are full of echoes, of memories, of associations – naturally. They have been out and about, on people's lips, in their houses, in the streets, in the fields, for so many centuries. And that is one of the chief difficulties in writing them today – that they are so stored with meanings, with memories, that they have contracted so many famous marriages. (*DM* 203)

This resonates with M. M. Bakhtin's commentary on words:

> All words have the 'taste' of a profession, a genre, a tendency, a party, a particular work, a particular person, a generation, an age group, the day and the hour. Each word tastes of the context and contexts in which it has lived its socially charged life; all words and forms are populated by intentions. (*DI* 293)

And as I reflected in Chapter 1, Bakhtin, like Woolf, contends that 'the word does not exist in a neutral and impersonal language (it is not, after all, out of a dictionary that the speaker gets his words!)' (*DI* 294). Susan

Stewart finds that Bakhtin's 'critique of "abstract objectivist" theories is directed to the following points: that such theories stabilise language at the expense of its real mutability and the creativity of its users'.[6] Although she is speaking only of Bakhtin, Woolf and Montaigne also critique abstractions and theories to similar ends. In Bakhtin's *Problems of Dostoevsky's Poetics*, Stewart finds that Bakhtin 'argues that identity is produced by speech, particularly through the contradictions of narrative' (Stewart 275). It is interesting that Bakhtin, like Montaigne, makes no distinction between 'language' and 'speech' (268), and also critiques 'system', noting that 'the semiotic character of culture is the result of concrete and dynamic historical processes, processes of tension and conflict inseparable from the basis of social and economic life' (271).

The importance of context is approached by Woolf in relation to making up new words, and finding that 'one cannot use a brand new word in an old language' because 'a word is not a single and separate entity, but is part of other words. It is not a word indeed until it is part of a sentence. Words belong to each other' (203). Questions abound regarding 'the English language as it is'. For how can we 'combine the old words in new orders so that they survive, so that they create beauty, so that they tell the truth? That is the question' (204). At this point, there are questions about the late sixteenth century in which Montaigne lived, 'when we were unlectured, uncriticized, untaught?': 'Is our Georgian literature a patch on the Elizabethan? . . . Is it words that are to blame?' Woolf's narrator suggests that the answer is a resounding yes. For words 'are the wildest, freest, most irresponsible, most unteachable of all things' (204). And they are placed in many dictionaries, with 'some half-a-million words all in alphabetical order. But can we use them? No, because words do not live in dictionaries, they live in the mind' (204–5); but, 'in moments of emotion when we most need words we find none. Yet there is a dictionary' (204). To emphasise where words truly reside, the narrator repeats this sentence three times – as we picture a nod from Bakhtin: 'But words do not live in dictionaries; they live in the mind.' Anthropomorphised by Woolf, words live in the mind 'variously and strangely, much as human beings live, by ranging hither and thither, by falling in love, and mating together. It is true that they are much less bound by ceremony and convention than we are' (205). And with that, Montaigne would wholeheartedly agree, for convention and ceremony are 'his great bugbears' (*CRI* 60), and words possess a freedom, a wildness, an inexplicable quality that cannot be mastered.

These words that live in the mind are etymological hybrids, for 'Royal words mate with commoners, English words marry French words, German words, Indian words, Negro words, if they have a fancy' (205).

Given their hybridity, 'they do not like to have their purity or their impurity discussed,' for 'there are no ranks or titles in their society' (205–6). Most importantly, words 'hate anything that stamps them with one meaning or confines them to one attitude, for it is their nature to change.' Key to Woolf's theorising of words is their multifaceted nature and their need for change:

> It is because the truth they try to catch is many-sided, and they convey it by being themselves many-sided, flashing this way and that. Thus they mean one thing to one person, another thing to another person; they are unintelligible to one generation, plain as pikestaff to the next. And it is because of this complexity that they survive. (*DM* 206)

This is a call to free words from the constraints of convention and ceremony, from rigid definitions, from simplicity, uniformity, for 'if we pin them down to one meaning, their useful meaning . . . they fold their wings and die.' Woolf's butterfly imagery, frequently linked with life and death, is clearly brought to mind with the 'pin', and her concern with maintaining the vitality of words makes her reluctant to negate their suggestiveness, to limit them in any way. This essay began with a significant change in title, one which expands the textual encounter, preserves the connection with its readers, empowers it readers and keeps words alive. Woolf's problems with definitions, categories, and the limitations and hierarchies inherent in genres have led to her constant attempts to subvert them. The second part of this chapter will investigate titles, Woolf's need to interrogate them, undermine them or simply change them, and why any kind of 'labelling', like naming, branding or entitling, calls forth issues of power, control and limitations.

Virginia Woolf clearly felt the need to change titles. But what is the impetus for her title changes? How many times do we invoke Woolf's multiple titles for her essays, her novels – and how many of us know how frequently she changed titles? Certain works stand out in this regard. *The Years* had nine or ten titles, and *Three Guineas* eleven or twelve. Was there always a new text, or did she maintain the text and by trial and error settle on her final title? How many times do we change titles for papers, proposals, books? And how many wish to change a title after publication?

Woolf's penchant for changing titles is evident because we have the good fortune to have the earlier drafts of many of her works, as well as letters, diaries and reading notes. This facility, however, is quickly disappearing with today's technology, although computerised 'versions' may be available; we lose the hand-written notes, the crossed-out words, the possible substitutions, and in essence, a good part of the creative process. Woolf's multiple titles also convey much that will be lost. Titles of all kinds are subject to scrutiny in her texts, whether they are used to attempt to define a work for its readers, or whether they are used to communicate the rank and stature of an individual in the many hierarchical institutions of various cultures. Titles of all kinds have also been problematic for Woolf because they certainly set limitations; simply the concept of naming or labelling indicates control, constraints, power. A title, as Woolf's narrator notes in 'On Re-reading Novels', 'gives us our bearings' (*M* 159). Titles can be said to provide her readers with some semblance of a roadmap – but one that Woolf would prefer to be slightly unreadable, almost inscrutable – thus empowering her readers to find or create their own trajectories; but titles, although they may be 'decapitated' and changed, are surely here to stay.

I will be examining Woolf's process of sequential entitling in the context of what we have concluded regarding her resistance to genre, to ranks, and to labels of all kinds. Her playing with genre, her search for some non-constricting 'labels' for her novels, and ultimately, her resistance to a rigid, stable text, make each new draft, in Edward Bishop's words, a 'new beginning',[7] an expression of her need to keep things open, to complicate them, to provide us with what many linguistic and feminist critics have called palimpsests, and what Donald Reiman has referred to as 'versioning'.[8] The need to undermine ranks, hierarchies and authorities, to transform things in order to keep them in motion, in flux, is significant in Woolf's works, and her changing titles serve to amplify that action. Montaigne also set the tone with his interest in and play with titles: 'The titles of my chapters do not always embrace their matter' (III:9, 761). According to Hugo Friedrich: '[Montaigne's] orientation toward linguistic criticism is behind this: no name can capture the wealth of a thing; the incongruence of title and content of an Essay is a symbol of the core theme of the *Essais* per se' (Friedrich 347). The title, according to Claire De Obaldia, is by definition 'a fragment which visibly stands out, exhibiting its definitional, centralising pretensions, subsuming the particular under the general' (De Obaldia 77). For Montaigne, the apparent lack of connection between titles and contents, until a distant and thus seemingly 'accidental' link appears, is not random. The title ultimately turns out to be one amongst the many features of the text, but its centralising claim is ironically marginalised, for 'the names of my chapters do not always encompass my subject-matter: often they merely indicate it by some token' (III:9, 761). This quotation is taken from Montaigne's essay, 'On Vanity', which Woolf's quotes in her own essay, 'Montaigne' (*CRI*). His commentary on naming, and on essay titles that obscure rather than clarify what they are supposed to define, obviously resonate with the lack of referentiality in language that both Woolf and Montaigne recognised. For the French writer, the name can only express the object incompletely. His additions to his texts were not meant as corrections to supersede earlier writing, since he never corrected his first thoughts, but created, with his additions, multiple viewpoints that ensured no authorised version. His titles also reflect that belief.

What are titles? And what is entitled to a title? How do titles of various kinds function? Are they roadmaps, blueprints of a type, major hints of what is to follow, a deceptive and misleading directive, or a gift of empowerment to readers, placing them in a position of control, of creativity? Do its functions align with the imposition of a name, category, brand or logo?

In John Fisher's article on titles, entitled 'entitling', his focus is on art and music titles, and he provides some interesting insights into the process of entitling – the complicated functions of titles – and these ideas certainly resonate with the examination of literary titles. We are all familiar with the influence of that little plate on the wall next to a painting. So do we skip it or check it out before we settle in front of the painting? It is always somewhat disappointing to approach it, only to find that the title is 'Untitled' or 'Number 9'. In speaking of Picasso's *Guernica*, there are of course a range of acceptable titles that might fit, and Fisher mentions a few possibilities: *The Bombing of a Basque Village* or *Luftwaffe Hell* (287). Not quite *Guernica*. With Magritte's picture of a pipe and the words 'this is not a pipe,' we see a picture of a pipe and that is the point. We also understand that publishers do not approve book titles that may jeopardise sales, and much time is spent selecting contemporary music and film titles due to marketing concerns.

Investigating the conceptual problems of titles, Fisher finds that they are always set in words – no matter what role they play – even if the title is a number or if it reads 'untitled'. Titles are names that we can refer to repeatedly – names which function as guides to interpretation, as ways to distinguish one work of art from another. They permit discourse about artworks of all kinds. Titles, as we know, tell us how to look at a work, how to listen to a musical piece, and for our purposes, some semblance of how to approach a written text. In Fisher's view: 'It is doubtful that the impact of *Guernica* could have been achieved without that verbal identification with the historical event of 1937 and the attendant social and emotional consequences' (292). Fisher points out that whether Matisse's 1905 painting of a head is sometimes called 'Madame Matisse' or, as happens more frequently, 'The Green Line', 'alters the meaning in a significant way; "Madame Matisse" is a portrait and "The

Green Line" is a purely fauvistic abstraction with the crucial emphasis on color' (292). We are being told how to view the work. 'Before Whistler, titles were more or less descriptive. Some were ambiguous and vague, but because art was so largely representational until the nineteenth century, titles primarily referred to what was represented' (295). Whistler's portrait of his mother was originally titled 'Arrangement in Grey and Black', and Fisher believes that the title makes a difference to our interpretation of the work. Is it a portrait or an arrangement of colours and forms? This distinction, according to Fisher, 'has everything to do with what interpretation I place upon it' (295).

Of course, if we are looking at Rauschenberg's 'Erased de Kooning Drawing', it both 'describes and identifies' (289). But there are disagreements about looking for titles to offer 'meaning', and Fisher gives his own opinion about Wittgenstein's assessment: '"Don't ask for meaning," cried Wittgenstein and his ilk, "Ask for use"' (289).

It is fascinating to question the influence titles have, and whether we get something different when listening to the same piece of music, depending on whether it is called the 'Jupiter Symphony' or 'Mozart's 41st' (289)? What titles clearly do is enable easier discourse about artworks. Titles also direct as well as limit the range of relationships. They call for responses, for interaction. Successful or not, they act as guides to interpretation.

For Virginia Woolf, many of the editorial decisions regarding some of her text's titles are recorded. Looking back to her earliest essay on the essay, which the then Virginia Stephen entitled: 'A Plague of Essays', we have her letter to Violet Dickinson, who had set her up with the editors of *Academy and Literature*; expressing her anger with these editors for changing her title without permission or notification, she stated that 'it means nothing, cut out a good half – and altered words . . . without giving me a chance to protest. I shouldn't so much mind if they hadn't clapped on my name in full at the end – to which I do object' (*LI* 181). The title had been changed to 'The Decay of Essay-Writing'.

Woolf's practice of multiple drafts, many with its own new title, permeated her writing practice from its beginning to her last works, 'Anon' and 'The Reader'. For Edward Bishop, these drafts should be considered 'new beginnings', with many also gaining a new title. A cursory reference to the changing titles of her works begins with the complicated history of *Melymbrosia* and her eventual first novel, *The Voyage Out*. Her second novel, *Night and Day* (1919), had the earlier title, 'Dreams and Realities', and *Jacob's Room, Mrs Dalloway, To the Lighthouse, A Room of One's Own, The Waves, The Years, Three Guineas* and *Between the Acts* all had a multitude of titles. A few examples will indicate the process of revision, of editorial decisions Woolf utilised. *Mrs Dalloway* had in its background the short stories, 'Mrs Dalloway in Bond St', and a sketch called 'The Prime Minister', but she wanted to call the novel 'At Home: or The Party'. Other titles include 'The Hours' and, in early stages, 'The Life of a Lady' and 'A Lady of Fashion'. The Clarissa in 'Mrs Dalloway in Bond Street' is, according to many critics, portrayed in a much harsher light than the character in the completed novel. The first title for *The Waves* was 'The Moths', a very significant symbol for Woolf, often associated with death and creation. She had to abandon it, however, when she realised that moths do not fly during the day, and finally wrote in her diary that she was writing 'to a rhythm and not to a plot', and would call it 'The Waves'. But her comments on many of her titles seemingly question them, asserting their provisional and tentative nature: In her diary, she refers to 'Waves or Moths or whatever it is to be called'. 'The Pargiters' was temporarily transformed into 'Here and Now', for Woolf 'thought it better'. 'It shows what I'm after and does not compete with the Herries Saga and the Forsyte saga and so on' (*DIV* 176). 'The Pargiters', of course, was followed by 'Here and Now', 'Music', 'Dawn', 'Sons and Daughters', 'Daughters and Sons', 'Ordinary People', 'The Caravan', 'Other People's Houses', and finally, *The Years*. For *Three Guineas*, Woolf thought about 'Professions for Women perhaps', 'The Open Door', 'Opening the Door', 'A Tap at the Door, or whatever it is', or even not remembering what she is using at one particular time: '"A Knock at the Door", (what's it's name?)'. Following this, 'Men are like that' was rejected as being 'too patently feminist' (*DIV* 77). She later speaks of dashing off the 'War (or whatever I call it)'. Brenda Silver's *Reading Notebooks* elaborate on some of Woolf's title choices for *Three Guineas*. Her mention, in the Monks House papers[9], of the title, 'The Next War', started around 1935, and the mention of the Brighton Conference – the Labour Party Conference in Brighton in October 1935 – 'spurred her to transform what was previously called 'On Being Despised' into 'The Next War'. At this conference, 'the pacifists headed by George Lansbury were resoundingly defeated' (Black 66), and her reading notebooks included the remark that 'men think war necessary.' Woolf describes the pacifists' defeat in a diary entry as 'the breaking of the dam between me and the new book' (*DIV* 346). By January 1936, a few months later, she decided to call it 'Answers to Correspondents', and by March 1936, 'Letter to an Englishman'. A week later it was to be called 'Two Guineas'. And finally, 'my war book' became *Three Guineas*.

In the process of writing drafts for *The Years*, she apparently ran into E. M. Forster on the steps of the London Library, where he had just come from a meeting at which the board had expressed the opinion that 'ladies were quite impossible' (*DIV* 300). Woolf's anger at this spurred her to thoughts of a book to be called 'on being despised', but she held back because *The Years* was 'dangerously near propaganda' and she could not write both at once (Hussey 388).[10] Of course, 'on being despised' became *Three Guineas*.

In Brenda Silver's 'Textual Criticism as Feminist Practice' in *Representing Modernist Texts*, she discusses Woolf's multiple drafts, the new versions of Woolf's texts that express much that was later deleted or transformed. Often, according to Silver, the early drafts were far more explicit in their social and political attitudes, and the reappraisal that took place in the 1970s and 1980s provoked questions as to which draft represented the author's 'final intention'. How do these differing titles express these different versions? We have Woolf's working titles, 'Melymbrosia', 'The Pargiters' and 'Pointz Hall', used by Leaska and DeSalvo, with 'Melymbrosia' considered by DeSalvo to be a 'submerged draft',[11] and Gilbert and Gubar calling it 'palimps-estic': a work 'whose surface designs conceal or obscure deeper, less accessible (less socially acceptable) levels of meaning'.[12] As Silver then suggests, 'we have come to accept that the multiple submerged texts in fact constitute the work we now know as *The Voyage Out*' (Silver, 'Textual Criticism', 204). The works are ultimately a composite – with sometimes contradictory aspects, indicating process over what used to be product. Do we also assess the titles of these works as being in process? Most interesting, according to Hans Zeller, is that 'even if all remains the same, a change in title indicates a different set of relation-ships among the elements in the text and hence a different semiotic system – and a different intention – than that signified by the same work with an alternate title.'[13] Silver suggests that 'the editorial choice of *Melymbrosia* or *The Pargiters* as title signifies the editors' critical intention to trace the ways in which the versions, while interconnected and three-dimensional, illustrate Woolf's sequentially changing inten-tions' (205). Silver treats the texts of 'Melymbrosia' and *The Voyage Out* as 'a single composite text', and the titles would have to be read intertextually, inclusively and relationally, thus negating any authori-tative 'authentic' version (206). The discussion of *The Pargiters* in Silver's article extends to:

> the etymological roots of the word, 'parget,' defined in the *English Dialect Dictionary* edited by Joseph Wright (who appears by name in the novel-essay version) as 'to plaster with cement and mortar,' or to 'whitewash,' and that 'pargeter' appears in the *Oxford English Dictionary* not only as 'a plasterer: a whitewasher' but by figurative extension 'one who glosses and smoothes

over' calls forth questions regarding Woolf as a 'pargeter' in her revisions, including the change of title from *The Pargiters* to *The Years*.[14]

I hope to complicate this issue by bringing in Montaigne's use of the word, 'plaster'. In speaking about 'appearances' and 'true intentions', Montaigne finds that 'we plaster over the fact: we know how we have said it and in what sense, and those present know it' and 'it is at the expense of our frankness and of the honor of our courage that we disown our thought, and seek rabbit-holes in falsehood in order to come to an agreement.' And he also finds that 'you must not consider whether your action or your word may have another interpretation; it is your true and sincere interpretation that you must henceforth maintain, whatever it costs you (III:10, 780). The business of 'pargeting' is clearly something that Montaigne wants to avoid. But for Woolf, the change of title, of a few words, results in 'a change in perspective, or intention' and 'a change of the relations within the work as a whole' (214).

The very act of revision is one of great complexity, and the selection of a title an intricate part of that process. The thought of the author's audience is clearly present, as the range of serial titles goes through changes. Editing and self-censorship – as Silver points out – are impossible to distinguish from one another; both, however, serve as ways to explore social and political critique, to decide how much to expose and how much to hide. What kind of title works best in each of these complex circumstances, and what is communicated or elided?

In her essay on Coleridge, entitled, 'The Man at the Gate' and written in September 1940, Woolf assesses why the name 'Coleridge' should not be the title of the work in question. The essay states that the man was Coleridge as De Quincey saw him, standing in a gateway:

> For it is vain to put the single word Coleridge at the head of a page – Coleridge the innumerable, the mutable, the atmospheric; Coleridge who is part of Wordsworth, Keats, Shelley; of his age and of our own; Coleridge whose written words fill hundreds of pages and overflow innumerable margins; whose spoken words still reverberate, so that as we enter his radius he seems not a man, but a swarm, a cloud, a buzz of words, daring this and that, clustering, quivering and hanging suspended. So little of this can be caught in any reader's net that it is well before we become dazed in the labyrinth of what we call Coleridge to have a clear picture before us – the picture of a man standing at a gate. (*DM* 104)

The description explains what entitling this work 'Coleridge' would lose, and what the reader clearly finds in the narrator's explanation of another title. The narrator discovers in the paralysed Coleridge 'an immense mass of quivering matter' (105), and finds that 'the great sentences pocketed with parentheses, expanded with dash after dash, break their walls under the strain of including and qualifying and suggesting all that Coleridge feels, fears and glimpses,' for often 'he is prolix to the verge of incoherence, and his meaning dwindles and fades to a wisp on the mind's horizon. Yet in our tongue-tied age, there is joy in this reckless abandonment to the glory of words' (*DM* 106).

Woolf's concern with maintaining the vitality of words makes her reluctant to 'refuse words their liberty' or 'pin them down to one meaning' (*DM* 206), as 'Craftsmanship' so clearly relates. This refusal to negate their suggestiveness serves, as the 'decapitation' of its title served, to expand the textual encounter, to keep her text and its connection with its reader, energised, alive. Her problems with titles, with definitions, and with the limitations and hierarchies inherent in genres, lead to her constant attempt to transform them – to find a less constrained mode of expression, and ultimately, to express the contradictions inherent in words, in life.

Notes

1. See S. P. Rosenbaum (1992), *Women & Fiction: The Manuscript Versions of A Room of One's Own*, Oxford: Blackwell, 3.
2. Ibid., xiii-xlii.
3. Jane Harrison [1903] (1991), *Prolegomena to the Study of Greek Religion*, Princeton, NJ: Princeton University Press.
4. Marcelin Pleynet was a writer, essayist, poet and managing editor of *Tel Quel* from 1962 to 1982. *Tel Quel* was an avant-garde magazine founded in 1960 by Philippe Sollers and Jean-Edern Hallier with a focus on linguistics, psychoanalysis and literature. The magazine represents twenty years of theoretical thinking by Kristeva, Barthes, Derrida, Genette and many of their contemporaries.
5. *The Colbert Report* is a satirical television show on *Comedy Central*, with Stephen Colbert, a political humorist who pretends to be a far-right Republican. His show critiques politics and the media.
6. Susan Stewart (1983), 'Shouts on the Street: Bakhtin's Anti-Linguistics', *Critical Inquiry* 10(2) (Dec.), 265–81. Stewart places the work of Bakhtin within a milieu of 'contradiction' (265), and finds his work not to be a linguistics, but, 'to use his word, a "metalinguistics"'.
7. Edward L. Bishop (1987), 'Metaphor and the Subversive Process of Virginia Woolf's Essays', *Style* 21(4) (Winter), 573–88.
8. Brenda Silver refers to Don Reiman's 'versioning' in (1991), 'Textual Criticism as Feminist Practice', in *Representing Modernist Texts*, ed. George Bornstein, Ann Arbor, MI: University of Michigan Press, 196. This article was published a year before (1992) *Women & Fiction: The Manuscript Versions of A Room of One's Own*, ed. S. P. Rosenbaum, Oxford: Blackwell.
9. One of many Library Special Collections of Virginia Woolf's papers, these were named after her home in Rodmell and are held at the University of

Sussex Library; see *Woolf Studies Annual* for a guide to Library Special Collections.

10. Mark Hussey (1995), *Virginia Woolf A–Z*, Oxford: Oxford University Press, 388.

11. Mitchell Leaska and Louise DeSalvo are editors of the manuscript versions of *Between the Acts* (Pointz Hall) and *The Voyage Out* (Melymbrosia), and their decision to use Woolf's working titles 'illustrates Woolf's sequentially changing intentions' (Silver 205).

12. See Sandra M. Gilbert and Susan Gubar (1979), *Madwoman in the Attic*, New Haven, CT: Yale University Press, 73.

13. See Hans Zeller (1975), 'A New Approach to Critical Constitution of Literary Texts', *Studies in Bibliography* 28, 240–1.

14. See Jane Marcus, '*The Years* as Greek Drama, Domestic Novel, and Gotterdammerung', and Mitchell A. Leaska, 'Virginia Woolf, the Pargeter: A Reading of *The Years*', both in *Bulletin of the New York Public Library* (1977), 80 (Winter): 280 and 172–4. Both are quoted by Brenda Silver in 'Textual Criticism as Feminist Practice', cited in note 8.

Part II

The Politics of Writing

Chapter 3

The Rhetoric of Performance in
A Room of One's Own

> But – were 'buts' beginning again? What did I mean by 'but' this time?
> *Women & Fiction*, Typescript Excerpts, Monks House Papers[1]

Woolf's *A Room of One's Own* both expresses and enacts its cultural critique by making certain that its readers not only see the significance of the women of their culture as 'outsiders', but also appropriate that position for themselves. My discussion, using Brecht's theory of performance, examines Woolf's rhetorical and narrative strategies – with a focus on the functioning of language and punctuation – to demonstrate how 'showing' the reader the process and calling attention to the constructed nature of the text serve to transform those readers – to get them to see and, ultimately, to critique those institutions that had become, in their entrenched familiarity, quite invisible.

I will begin near the end of *A Room of One's Own* with a passage not usually highlighted, but one which permits Woolf to take her cultural critique in a multitude of directions. Here, one of her narrators responds to the aridity of Mr. A's new novel:

> But . . . I had said 'but' too often. One cannot go on saying 'but.' One must finish the sentence somehow, I rebuked myself. Shall I finish it, 'But – I am bored!' But why was I bored? (104)

After five 'buts' in as many sentences, the reader of *A Room of One's Own* is not so much interested in why the narrator is bored, as to why she keeps repeating 'but'. Why does this essay, which, incidentally, also begins its first and last sentences with the word 'but', seem to reverberate with its significance? Indeed, its sentences do get finished – but with enough equivocation for 'but', along with 'perhaps' and 'might', to become, inevitably, the expected conclusion – or rather, the lack of conclusion. In fact, throughout this essay, as the above passage conveys, Woolf's narrators inform their readers of their difficulties and speculate about the forms and methods used to express their experiences.

That the first word of *A Room of One's Own* is 'but' does not seem mere chance, for Woolf's narrator in 'The Modern Essay' declares that the essay 'should lay us under a spell with its first word' (*CRI* 211). One does wonder, however, what kind of 'spell' is cast upon the reader when 'but' not only begins a text, but is also, in the immediately established dialogue, transferred to the reader's lips by the narrator? By giving this line to the reader, the narrator places herself 'in the position of the one asked' (*DIV* 361), thus transferring a sense of uncertainty, as well as resistance, to the reader. Interestingly, the varied definitions of 'but' – including 'except', 'outside' and 'on the contrary', to name just a few[2] – seem to echo the marginal position of women in our culture; and quite significantly, several of these words are used in *A Room of One's Own* to describe the woman 'walking down Whitehall, when from being the natural inheritor of that civilization, she becomes, *on the contrary, outside of it, alien and critical*' (101; emphasis added).

With the constant intrusion of 'but', the text simultaneously resonates with the multiple interruptions in women's lives and the resultant open-ness created by these breaks. It seems, very simply, that 'but' will always negate the state of boredom which Woolf's narrator both describes and questions, for 'but' refuses that boredom by leaving things open, creating new possibilities; this coincides, of course, with what Woolf considers a necessary vitality, the essence of life. 'But', in its ambiguity, functions as a connective, as a way of continuing and extending, although it also resists that continuity, cuts things off, and most importantly, negates what was said before its appearance. One can assume that something preceded the narrator's opening word, as one always assumes with 'but' that something will follow.

'But', in its linkage with the marginality of women, serves to enact their exclusion and oppression with its strategically placed interrup-tions. Strolling through Oxbridge, thinking about 'that wild flash of imagination' (7) in the essays of Lamb, the narrator's thoughts move her to speculate about Lamb's thinking regarding Milton's possible revision of *Lycidas*, as well as her own thinking about Thackeray's alterations to *Esmond*, and whether those revisions improved the style or the meaning: '*But* then one would have to decide what is style and what is meaning, a question which – *but* here I was actually at the door which leads into the library itself. I must have opened it, for instantly there issued, like a guardian angel barring the way' (7; emphasis added). The narrator's quest is now interrupted by 'but', as her path was previously intercepted and diverted by the Beadle. 'But', by interrupting the sentence as well as her entrance to the library, also interrupts her thoughts and imaginings, her intellectual curiosity and, most importantly, her desire. What follows 'but' is the fact of her exclusion. Her imagination shrinks into the background, as does her all-important freedom. This imaginative freedom, although negated, is, as Wolfgang Iser asserts in another context, still on the page – still visible to the reader and thus still a viable option (169).

Also visible to the reader, and explicitly foregrounded by Woolf's various narrators throughout the text, are ellipses and parentheses; interrupting and intruding themselves into sentences, they call attention to the constructed nature of the text and to the process of writing. In this self-conscious acknowledgement of text as text, there is an implicit recognition of the presence of an audience, of readers. For these readers, an ellipsis may indicate a withholding, a pause or an omission; it may also express a leap, without logical connections, from one topic to another. This provides the readers with an opportunity to participate, consciously and unconsciously, in the creation of their text – and, as Iser suggests, to fill in the blanks (168). The blanks are spaces of indeterminacy, of possible repression, of unconscious desire, and become spaces for self-conscious questioning as the narrator, for example, poses questions regarding truth and illusion:

> Why, if it was an illusion, not praise the catastrophe, whatever it was, that destroyed illusion and put truth in its place? For truth . . . those dots mark the spot where, in search of truth, I missed the turning up to Fernham. (15)

And so the ellipses in *A Room of One's Own*, as Shari Benstock suggests, are used 'to signal a falling back or turning away from the socially constructed opposition of truth and illusion within Western thinking, a moment of contradiction and confusion'[3] (124).

Woolf's narrator follows this confusing and attention-getting device by giving her readers some of the evidence she finds during the problematic nature of her quest. She provides varying perspectives which display the contingent nature of one's observations and conclusions. In this case, the houses she observes are 'dim and festive now with their red windows in the dusk, but raw and red and squalid, with their sweets and their boot-laces, at nine o'clock in the morning' (15). Here all is contingent upon time. This questioning of truth and illusion is also replicated as the ellipsis blurs textual boundaries. This mark of punctuation, the ellipsis, is talked about as if the dots which structure it were really marks on the road. And the statement that 'no conclusion was found on the road to Headingly' (16) similarly blurs boundaries and calls attention to the text as a construct, as readers find themselves questioning that 'a conclusion' might be found on the road. The narrator's pursuit of truth continues with a trip to the counter of the British Museum Library, where an examination of the catalogue provokes a very different explanation of her next ellipsis: '. . . . . the five dots here indicate five separate minutes of stupefaction, wonder and bewilderment' (26). Her readers may also experience surprise at this confusing interruption of the narrative, as they are addressed directly with the question: 'Are you aware that you are, perhaps, the most discussed animal in the universe?' This direct question serves to distance her readers in order to gain their attention, as she continues to investigate her inability to capture the 'truth' about women.

Along with the ellipsis, the parenthesis also functions to attract as well as distract her readers by its intrusion into the text. Working as an aside, the parenthesis can add something new that may seem out of place, or abruptly change the direction of the thoughts being conveyed; in another sense, it makes what had been contextualised in a certain way suddenly become the context for the newly added parenthetical statement. One is reminded of the 'Time Passes' section of *To the Lighthouse*, where catastrophes are scattered, parenthetically, to place them in the context of another kind of destruction; that they are mentioned as Kafka might mention them – so very nonchalantly – also serves to foreground them. This sometimes self-conscious disruption of the narrator's 'train of thought' (4) also serves to disrupt the thinking of her readers, moving them off the path as the narrator was moved off the path by the Beadle.

These interruptions by 'but' and by the ellipses and parentheses serve as a partial solution to the narrator's boredom with the discourse of Mr. A's and Mr. B's writings. The compartmentalisation of Mr. B's mind seemed to deny access to his feelings, and in his sentences, 'it is the power of suggestion that one most misses' (105); this suggestiveness is a call for openness, for contradictions and a certain wildness. The 'smooth lawns' (9) of the men's colleges, perceived as lacking this wildness, are compared to the 'wild unkempt grasses' (20) of Fernham, for the roughness and disorder hold more interest. Her boredom is a critique of this smoothness, of the hard and the barren; these qualities are aligned with cultural traditions that exclude women, with language and forms that cannot express women's lives, and with a rigidity that negates creativity.

There is much that acts to counter the rigidity and fixity of patriarchal institutions, the lifeless inscriptions of members of those institutions, and the 'spirit of peace' which prevails when one stays 'on the paths', or 'in the courts and quadrangles of Oxbridge' (6). For the narrator, trespassing, crossing boundaries or stepping on the forbidden turf is precipitated by a degree of excitement and by 'the mysterious property' of ideas; these thoughts 'flashed hither and thither, set up such a wash and tumult of ideas that it was impossible to sit still' (5). When intercepted and chased from the turf on to the gravel, however, these thoughts and ideas – imaged by Woolf's narrator as 'my little fish' (another definition of 'but') – are sent into hiding. Using 'but' in exchange for 'fish' and sending it 'into hiding' reiterates the banishment of the imagination, for in getting rid of this mode of interruption one smoothes out the text as one smoothes out the turf. This sequestering of ideas, of imagination, where 'the roughness of the present seemed smoothed away' (6), is equated with a dull and lifeless quality. The narrator's experience upon passing the chapel door also reflects this lifelessness: 'Even the sorrow of Christianity sounded in that serene air more like the recollection of sorrow than sorrow itself; even the groanings of the ancient organ seemed lapped in peace' (8).

Again we have a kind of 'peacefulness' linked with lifelessness. The emotion lacking in this serene setting could be found by trespassing on the turf, or by visiting the gardens of Fernham which were 'not orderly', but 'wild and open', and 'windblown and waving' (17). To counter this stifling of ideas, imagination and creativity, *A Room of One's Own* performs the essayistic – sanctioning mobility, wandering and the crossing of boundaries. As the narrator wanders, strolling past many magnificent buildings, she speculates about the 'unending stream of gold and silver' which must have flowed, and continues to flow, in order to maintain all of this. This 'foundation of gold and silver' is linked with 'the pavement laid solidly over the wild grasses' (10); and the wild grasses are linked with the life at the women's college. The desire for mobility and all that it engenders is evident in the deprivation of this activity; even the fact that there was no 'walking tour' (54) for women contributed to the stifling of their thoughts and imaginings.

There is an oscillation between the 'rambling' (83) and 'strolling' (6) of the narrators – and their minds – and the constraints that try to maintain the nineteenth century's notion that women be silent and still. Subverting society's rule of limiting them to the gravel path, these women must take the wrong turn, duck around the corner, and let the line of their thoughts 'dip into the stream' (5). This activity is both their resistance and their tactic for survival. The desire of a narrator to 'expose what was in her mind to the air' (19) expresses her need for freedom. As the narrator thinks about the mysterious qualities of the mind and just how it functions, she simultaneously enacts this process before her readers; her readers/audience watch her as she thinks about the mind thinking, and her tentative conclusion regarding this state of the mind is 'that it seems to have no single state of being'. Most importantly, it 'is always altering its focus, and bringing the world into different perspectives' (101).

In Woolf's *A Room of One's Own*, its narrators attempt to reveal the inner workings of their minds. Filled as it is with many dialogues which often engage the readers, Woolf's narrators will, without claiming to know anything with certainty, show as well as tell, as the audience joins in on this speculative process.

> I am going to develop in your presence as fully and freely as I can the train of thought which led me to think this. Perhaps if I lay bare the ideas, the prejudices, that lie behind this statement you will find that they have some bearing upon women and some upon fiction. . . . when a subject is highly controversial – and any question about sex is that – one cannot hope to tell the truth. One can only show how one came to hold whatever opinion one does hold. (4)

Woolf's narrator constantly speculates about the reader's response to her assigned topic, and about her effectiveness with the assignment. In her attempt to 'show how one came to hold the opinions one holds' (4), to show the process of her thinking, Woolf's self-consciousness regarding language, punctuation, changes of narrative voice and changes of scene becomes a prominent strategy. This self-consciousness produces an interesting effect on her readers, for it both engages them and distances them, continuing the oscillating movement that repudiates – in yet another way – the rigidity and fixity of forms, institutions, people, and the language used to construct them. In this instance, the oscillation repudiates a fixed stance, a fixed perspective from which we can judge and formulate our opinions.

This distancing of the reader has some resonance with Bertolt Brecht's 'estrangement effect'. One of the important goals of Brecht's 'Epic Theatre', which relates to many of Woolf's novels[4] and particularly to *A Room of One's Own* and *Three Guineas*, is to have her audience discover the conditions of life. Sallie Sears sees aspects of Brecht's 'Epic Theatre' in the context of the audience of Miss La Trobe's play in *Between the Acts*, and finds that 'it is predicated upon the assumption (so crucial to modernists like Brecht, Artaud, Peter Weiss) that an audience that sees deplorable truths, hitherto unconscious, hidden, or denied, will not only deplore, but seek to abolish the circumstances that brought them into being' (Sears 229). This takes place through an interruption of happenings (as Woolf's narrator is interrupted when she opens the door of the library, or the text is interrupted by a parenthetical comment or a reference to punctuation). The narrator also periodically interrupts her own narrative in order to undermine the illusion her audience has accepted. To accomplish this, the narrator simply points out to the reader that she is creating scenes and fictionalising, thus causing them to acknowledge that the impervious boundary between fact and fiction is not so easily discernible:

> As I have said already that it was an October day, I dare not forfeit your respect and imperil the fair name of fiction by changing the season and describing lilacs hanging over garden walls, crocuses, tulips, and other flowers of spring. Fiction must stick to facts, and the truer the facts the better the fiction – so we are told. Therefore it was still autumn and the leaves were still yellow and falling, if anything, a little faster then before, because it was now evening (seven twenty-three *to be precise*) and a breeze (from the south-west *to be exact*) had risen. (16; emphasis added)

The narrator obviously over-emphasises the precision and exactitude of her fictionalising, in order to call even more attention to the problematic nature of factuality. By self-consciously calling attention to the strategy of fictionalising, Woolf is confronting her audience with the problematic nature of such dichotomising.

As Woolf foregrounds this playing with 'fact' and 'fiction', she frequently makes visual – as is the case of the ellipses and parentheses – all those places where the text refers to itself as a text; all of these, in a Brechtian sense, both engage and distance the reader. Relating Brecht's 'Epic Theatre' to *Jacob's Room*, Edward L. Bishop finds that the aim is 'to make a spectator use his or her critical sense' and that 'the process of showing must itself be shown' (157). Bishop also notes that Walter Benjamin's assessment of Brecht can be applied to Woolf, for she is also less interested in the 'development of actions' than in the 'representation of conditions' (Benjamin 150). Woolf's rhetorical strategies also seem to echo Brecht's 'Epic Theatre', for the oscillation I refer to in *A Room of One's Own* seems to resonate with Brecht's aim of 'detachment' and 'reorientation' (Willett 1967, 170–7).

Like the songs, captions and exposed stagecraft of Brecht's 'Epic Theatre', Woolf's use of 'but', the ellipses, the parentheses and the other self-conscious references to the text function to impair the illusion. Calling attention to the constructed nature of the text, to words as words, and to what may have been withheld, serves to distance the audience – to make them, at times, spectators or outsiders, thus enabling them to critique those institutions which continue to structure and have power over their lives, and perhaps to enact some necessary resistance.

Notes

1. See earlier references to 'but' in the typescript excerpts from *A Room of One's Own* in S. P. Rosenbaum (1992), *Women & Fiction*, 189. Woolf's

use of 'but' has been discussed in differing contexts by Bowlby, 17–18; Rosenman, 93; and Bishop, 'Metaphor and the Subversive Process of Virginia Woolf's Essays', 574.

2. 'But', as a noun, also refers to a fish, which may fit in with Woolf's fishing metaphor; a 'but' in Scotland refers to the outer room, especially the kitchen, of a cottage; and, of course, to 'butt' is to thrust against (*OED*). All of these resonate in various ways with Woolf's usage.

3. Benstock finds that the 'ellipsis is not merely a recurrent textual feature of *Three Guineas*, it constitutes the primary structuring device of the text, joining political argument to the rhetorical-grammatical form through which it is elaborated' (124). See her chapter, 'Ellipsis: Figuring Feminisms in *Three Guineas*', in *Textualizing the Feminine* (123–62). Bowlby also discusses ellipses in a variety of Woolf's works, in 'The Dotted Line', *Virginia Woolf: Feminist Destinations* (160–70).

4. For other discussions relating Brecht's 'Epic Theatre' to Woolf's novels, see Bishop, 'The Subject in *Jacob's Room*', 147–75; Johnston, 61–75; and Sears, 212–35.

Chapter 4

Interrogating 'Wildness'

Alas, laid on the grass how small, how insignificant this thought of mine looked. . . . But however small it was, it had, nevertheless, the mysterious property of its kind – put back into the mind, it became at once very exciting, and important; and as it darted and sank, and flashed hither and thither, set up such a wash and tumult of ideas that it was impossible to sit still. It was thus that I found myself walking with extreme rapidity. Instantly a man's figure rose to intercept me. . . . His face expressed horror and indignation. Instinct rather than reason came to my help; he was a Beadle; I was a woman. This was the *turf*; there was the *path*. Only the Fellows and Scholars are allowed here; the *gravel* is the place for me. . . . Once, presumably, this quadrangle with its *smooth lawns*, its massive buildings, and the chapel itself was marsh, too, where the *grasses waved* and the swine rooted. . . . Certainly, as I strolled around the court, the foundation of gold and silver seemed deep enough; the pavement laid solidly over the *wild grasses*.

Virginia Woolf, *A Room of One's Own*[1]

Turf. Gravel path. Smooth lawns. Wild grasses. Virginia Woolf's *A Room of One's Own* not only establishes territory, possession, boundaries, and the marking of ground but also qualifies this territorial imperative with its self-conscious fictionalisation of 'Fernham' and 'Oxbridge'. Woolf's narrator reveals that 'lies will flow from my lips, but there *may perhaps* be some truth mixed up with them; it is for you to seek out this truth and to decide whether any part of it is worth keeping' (4; emphasis added). Of course, the reader is advised to ascertain the value of what is being imparted. But as my epigraph reveals, the reader is being provided with more than the rudimentary lay of the land, for the grounds of Fernham and Oxbridge will soon become the platform for an extremely exciting and complicated metaphorical adventure.

This gendered landscape – the 'smooth lawns' of the men's colleges and the 'wild grasses' of the women's colleges – holds within, in its sedimentary layers, the archeological remains of its ancient past. Exploring

this geological and textual site, readers conjure up thoughts of the artificial, the natural, exclusion, concealment, deprivation, order, chaos,
fertility, death and so much more; this rich landscape conceals the foundations, the roots and the origins of this complex ground on which the
social, political and economic events of the past have made their marks,
developed their cultures and created their so-called 'civilisations'. Here,
the metaphorics of both vegetative and animalistic states transport the
reader to sites that both express and enact a dialectic of stasis and mobility, sterility and fertility, compliance and resistance. And within these
contradictory states, endemic in Woolf's writings, one finds a pervasive
'wildness', frequently hidden but periodically bursting through the
façades that serve to contain them – to deny them and to resist exposing
any clear point of origin.

It is to Virginia Woolf's complex use of the words 'wild', 'wildness',
'savage' and 'barbaric' that I turn in this chapter, to explore how she
takes her readers on this metaphoric journey – encompassing ancient
myths, colonialism, patriarchal rule, commercial power – for, as
Montaigne has written: 'all subjects are linked with one another' (III:5,
668). The words 'wildness' and 'wild', so frequently connected with
'women', the 'mind', 'thinking', 'ideas', the 'essayistic' and 'movement',
will be linked with 'grasses', ' root systems', the modes of 'growth' and
'movement', and ultimately, as 'words' – for, as Woolf's narrator points
out in 'Craftsmanship', 'words are the wildest, freest, most irresponsible, most unteachable of all things' (*DM* 204).

In its various *OED* meanings, 'wild', in all its varied forms, conveys
something living or growing in its natural state; not domesticated or
cultivated; savage; primitive; unkempt; not easily restrained or regu-
lated; not submitting to control; violently disturbed; characterised by a
lack of moral restraint; in a state of mental excitement; and/or a state
of disorder, or just simply 'uncivilised'. And yet, all of these are surely
somehow pertinent to what Woolf conveys, especially when one considers the gendering of the smooth, manicured lawns of Oxbridge, and
the 'wild wavy grasses' of Fernham. The social, economic and political
underpinnings of these landscaping distinctions, made explicit in *A
Room of One's Own* but pervasive in all Woolf's writings, function to
interrogate the problematic nature of both the 'wild' and the 'civilised;'
in today's world, where torture, rape and 'conventional' killing, as
opposed to the increased killing by 'drones', fill the news each day, the
difficulties of distinguishing the so-called 'civilised' from the savage and
the 'barbaric' is no simple task. I began with *A Room of One's Own*,
but will venture back to Woolf's early diary entries and her letters, and
to *The Voyage Out*, *Between the Acts* and other relevant writings, in

order to show how this multifaceted subject of 'wildness', and especially 'wild grass', functions metaphorically, to expose, indict or praise colonialism, fascism, social purity movements, prostitution, militarism and gender inequity – many of these, of course, overlapping and related to one another.

Looking back to my epigraph, to the narrator's thought, her idea, the idea that had 'sent [her] so audaciously trespassing' (*AROO* 6), we now enter a scene that serves to show the readers the demise of this creative endeavour, the one that squelched her idea and 'sent it into hiding'; it is, of course, a response to the experience of the territorial displacement of women at Oxbridge and so many other places in her world. Here, readers are transported to mythical sites, to places of the Other, places where they witness the possibilities for the release of a creative spirit that has been heretofore denied, both within the text and, perhaps – as Woolf would say, in their own lives.

Exploring the sedimentary layers of this land, a geological field evoking the ancient, the primeval, and all that has accumulated over the ages finally to create the present, one acknowledges the constant flow of gold and silver from kings, queens, nobles, merchants and manufacturers that supports this powerful institution. One also acknowledges an internal primeval presence concealed by this so-called 'civilisation', by Oxbridge; significantly, in the past, 'its smooth lawns, its massive buildings, and the chapel itself was marsh, too, where the grasses waved and the swine rootled' (*AROO* 9). Most significantly, we see the gendering of this particular landscape. The surfaces one walks on, the spaces one inhabits, the sense of belonging or exclusion – clearly suggested by where women are 'placed' in an inequitable world – all function metaphorically, in myriad ways, in all of Virginia Woolf's writings; but only one of these experiences – exposing the relegation of women to a specific and undesirable surface – to the only kind of 'placement' women could attain at Oxbridge, has achieved iconic status. Being 'turfed', a British slang term for being 'ejected' or 'displaced', is forever etched in the minds of the multitudes of readers of *A Room of One's Own* – women and/or Others – who have also been 'turfed' in some way in their own lives, since those 'gravel paths' of the early twentieth century have expanded, in the context of the twenty-first century, to include new and infinitely more horrific incarnations. On the grounds of 'whatever the college might happen to be', where one of Woolf's narrators has difficulty interpreting the gesticulations of the Beadle, 'a curious-looking *object*, in a cut-away coat and evening shirt' (*AROO* 6; emphasis added), the narrator has assertively taken back – owned – her designated surface, for 'the gravel is the place for me.'

In thinking about the varied meanings of 'gravel' – with 'bewildering' and 'mysterious' amongst them – the narrator's state of mind, her inability to identify the college, her difficulty interpreting the Beadle's gestures extend a mode of freedom to this surface material, opening this specific type of 'path' to a variety of politically inflected trajectories – and perhaps gathering some necessary resistance. The narrator is not so much concerned with the gravel but with the personal effect of this 'protection of their turf, which has been rolled for 300 years in succession', for 'they had sent [her] little fish into hiding' (*AROO* 6). This 'little fish', of course, is the little idea she had laid on the grass, the one that when 'put back into the mind' had very significantly 'sent her trespassing': this 'little idea', filled with mystery, is described as 'exciting' and 'important', as 'it darted and sank, and flashed hither and thither, and set up such a tumult of ideas that it was impossible to sit still' (*AROO* 5). The business of 'stillness' seems to revert to the subject of Martha Vicinus's book on Victorian and early twentieth-century women, entitled *Suffer and Be Still*,[2] and deals with the Ellis etiquette books that extol the virtue of the immobility of women. The 'sitting still' part will play a larger role in this discussion as we move forward, for it takes us back to the resistance of the 'essayistic', to voyaging – within and without – and the transformations that living – and writing – entail.

This gravel, made from crushed stone, was clearly uncomfortable, but

> the roughness of the present seemed smoothed away; the body seemed contained in a miraculous glass cabinet through which no sound could penetrate, and the mind, freed from any contact with facts (unless one trespassed on the turf again), was at liberty to settle down upon whatever meditation was in harmony with the moment. (*AROO* 6)

This meditation, however, was soon to be denied, destroyed or simply eliminated, for entrance to the library was refused, the territory once again strictly protected, and the narrator's decision to pass the chapel – to remain 'outside' these venerated spaces – suddenly made sense, for 'the outside of these magnificent buildings is often as beautiful as the inside' (8). But there was much more going on here, for as she 'leant against the wall the University indeed seemed a sanctuary in which are preserved rare types which would soon be obsolete if left to fight for existence on the pavement of the Strand' (8). Were they up to such a challenge?

In Oxbridge, the 'high domes and pinnacles can be seen, like a sailing-ship always voyaging never arriving'. These high domes of the men's colleges, these forbidden spaces, represented a 'sailing-ship *always* voyaging *never* arriving' (9; emphasis added) – a contradictory construct expressing stasis and tension – but were significantly 'lit up at night and visible for miles' (9) to display their orderly, albeit 'still', self. This seems indicative of the 'stationary voyage', as Gilles Deleuze[3] refers to it, and reflects Montaigne's views of those who travel only to seek what they left behind – therefore not 'seeing' the differences, the new, the foreign, but staying with the familiar: 'they think they are out of their element when they are out of their village' but 'most of them take the trip only for the return' (Montaigne III:9, 754). Looking back at the 'stillness', the immobility imposed upon women, here, in this fictionalised place, the impetus is to change the season for the readers, to move from 'the October day' to spring, with 'lilacs hanging over the garden walls', but the narrator must stay with 'facts', and so 'the leaves were still yellow and falling' and 'it was now evening (seven twenty-three *to be precise*) and a breeze (from the southwest *to be exact*) had risen' (16; emphasis added). The over-emphasis on the precision of her statement serves to keep the readers aware of the fictiveness of this setting.

Under these massive buildings of Oxbridge there was 'once' a 'marsh' – and interestingly, but not surprising for Woolf's words, another word for 'marsh' is 'morass' – a place of confusion not unlike the 'gravel' depicted earlier; all of these locations, along with their characteristics, are aligned with women. Woolf's letters and diary entries are filled with references to marshes, the place of the 'will o the wisps', as she describes in this letter to Violet Dickinson: 'But at night a whole flower bed of fitful lighthouses blooms' (*LI* 307) for the will o the wisps always radiated lights. She places them in *Night and Day* where, to Katherine, 'the book became a wild dance of the will o the wisps – without form or continuity, without coherence, even, or any attempt to make a narrative' (*ND* 43). And in her giving the title of 'The Complete Insider' to George M. Trevelyan, when he became Master of Trinity College, Cambridge, in 1940, she added that Insiders 'do a great service like Roman roads. But they avoid the forests & the will o the wisps' (*DV* 333). The forests and the will-o'-the-wisps clearly represent the 'outsiders'.

This primeval space, of course, had been transformed, for it took 'infinite labour' to place 'the grey blocks . . . in order one on top of another . . . and the masons were busy for centuries up on that roof' . . . and 'somebody poured gold and silver out of a leathern purse into their ancient fists' (*AROO* 9). It is my purpose to look under these 'magnificent' buildings, to delve into the primeval, to examine the mythological significance of women and their ancient linkage with 'wildness', while exposing, throughout Woolf's writings, the social, economic and political links of women and differing forms of the 'wild'. I will focus on their frequent connection with 'wild grasses', to show how the pervasive use of the word 'wild' in all of its varied contexts functions to involve its readers with the broader implications of being 'placed', 'rooted', or constrained by the 'civilised' patriarchal culture, and the call for and enactment of resistance to these constraints. The 'wild unkempt grasses' (20) of Fernham and the 'smooth lawns' of the quadrangles of a fictitious Oxbridge conjure up thoughts of the natural as opposed to the artificial, of exclusion and territoriality, of the savage and the barbaric as opposed to the civilised, of disorder opposed to order, of discomfort to comfort, the mad to the sane, and the underlying traditions and conventions that support these conflictual forces. As I explore these oppositions, clearly marked in some contexts, unclear in others, one finds, on a continuum of sorts, evidence that language, labels and categories are interrogated, and that the focus is somewhat blurred. They are not dichotomised, not either/or contentions. That Woolf would not want these terms to be clearly defined, robbed of their mutability, their freedom – spatially or definitionally – is supported by the consistent re-contextualisation of certain words throughout the corpus of her writings.

Looking back to her novel, *To the Lighthouse* (1927), one notes the linkage of 'wild flowing grasses' and women, and simultaneously, the exclusion of men:

> the hoary Lighthouse, distant, austere, in the midst; and on the right, as far as the eye could see, fading and falling, in the soft low pleats, the green sand dunes with the wild flowing grasses on them, which always seemed to be running away into some moon country, uninhabited of men. (*TL* 23)[4]

What began as a questioning of this metaphor – and Woolf's use of metaphor – became an investigation of the political implications of its use and its linkage to other significant and intricately related political issues of the past that were problematic in the early twentieth century – and, as we recognise, are still problematic today; I include colonisation, racism, eugenics, social purity movements, and the varied modes of the exclusion and degradation of women, of the Other. I have argued that the 'peacefulness' related in *A Room of One's Own* is a 'peace' linked with lifelessness, with stasis, and that the 'wild and open', the gardens of Fernham, were 'not orderly' (17), the 'waving grasses' not still, and that *A Room of One's Own* performs the essayistic by sanctioning mobility, wandering and trespassing. I have also noted that the 'unending stream of gold and silver' – maintaining the kind of landscape the narrator strolls by – enables the men's colleges to control and transform the surrounding surfaces; as noted above, this 'foundation of gold and silver' has links with 'the pavement laid solidly over the wild grasses' (10). With women consistently connected to grasses, and especially 'wild' grasses, and the powerful institutions linked with 'smooth' and 'hard' lawns, manicured and mowed with regularity, we can assess the 'pavement laid solidly over the wild grasses' as indicating the crushing of women's lives and their thoughts, as well as their creative spirit. Reinforcing this image, Woolf's narrator expands the metaphor slightly in comparing how 'the kings and queens and nobles bearing sacks of gold and silver which they shovelled into the earth' for so long with 'how the great financial magnates of our own time came and laid cheques and bonds' (20) in the treasuries of these men's colleges.

After the decidedly inferior dinner at Fernham, and the knowledge of the gold and silver sustaining the colleges of Oxbridge, a significant question arises regarding Fernham: 'what lies beneath its gallant red brick and the wild unkempt grasses of the garden?' (20).

It is interesting to note that these 'wild unkempt grasses', their linkage with women, with nourishment, with growth, have the ability to grow where nothing else will grow. In *A Room of One's Own*, one finds the letter 'I' shading out what may be woman, for the shadow of Alan obliterates Phoebe. This 'I', equated with Alan, is now the giant beech tree, which casts a great shadow, ensuring that 'nothing will grow there' (104). With minimal nourishment available, however, the wild grasses exude life, as many of these 'wild grasses' multiply with 'rhizomatic' growth, a rooting mechanism that offers great metaphoric and political significance. Questions abound regarding the kinds of 'rooting' they have, whether single taproots or multiple roots reach down into the earth, and the direction of their growth. The horizontal and branching nature of rhizomatic growth is a subject that Gilles Deleuze and Félix Guattari utilise in many of their works; in *A Thousand Plateaus: Capitalism and Schizophrenia*,[5] they posit that 'writing has nothing to do with signifying. It has to do with surveying, mapping, even realms that are yet to come' (4–5). In their challenge to 'the tree' as 'the image of the world, or the root the image of the world tree', or 'the book as the image of the world' (5–6), they move on to the significance of the 'rhizome' and describe it as 'a subterranean stem absolutely different from roots and radicles. Bulbs and tubers are rhizomes' (6). Focusing on 'wild grasses', one finds that many grow in 'marshes', their 'rhizomatic' qualities conjuring up questions regarding roots and the complexities of that word.

The complexity of 'roots', the differing contexts, whether we are 'rooted', stable, planted, settled, anchored, are repeatedly used to question 'roots' – and 'origins' – and several of those terms, such as 'settled', 'anchored' 'planted', and 'rooted', are also used in Woolf's writings to allude to a fixed mode of being, amongst other things. These multiple meanings of being 'rooted', 'grounded', also relate the rhizomatic growth processes to politics and to language. One finds in Woolf's 'Street Haunting' a metaphorical use, as they approach a door: 'We are in danger of digging deeper than the eye approves; we are impeding our passage down the smooth stream by catching at some branch or root' (*DM* 23). But the dangers and risks are encouraged.

I argued in the last chapter that Virginia Woolf attempts, in her narrative and rhetorical strategies, to unsettle her readers, and perhaps, in the context of the 'essayistic' and 'wildness', to keep her readers moving, on new and challenging trajectories, paths to new creative outlets. The 'rhizomatic' growth, as utilised by Deleuze and Guattari, exhibits a non-hierarchical system, with horizontal branching, where growth can begin at any point, with no definitive place of 'origin'. That most 'wild grasses' are 'rhizomatic' is most interesting for this study. What are these 'wild grasses' that have been linked to women in so many of Woolf's works – grasses that have thousands of varieties, some characterised by their ability to grow where nothing else will, with other grasses that have links with orchids, with plants that grow from bulbs and tubers? What is it about the growth of these special plants that has relevance for the exploration of women and the 'wild' in a multitude of contexts? The work of Deleuze and Guattari on the 'rhizome' illuminates Woolf's use of this particular metaphor, with her use of 'wild grasses' placed in opposition to 'manicured lawns' – for women have been ejected from these smooth, comfortable places. For Deleuze and Guattari, 'the rhizome is a subterranean stem,' generally plants with bulbs and tubers, but 'burrows and rats' are included along with such diverse forms as potatoes, couchgrass, crabgrass or the weed', and 'there are diverse modes of coding (biological, political, economic) that bring into play not only different regimes of signs, but also states of things of differing status' (7). Importantly, the term 'rhizome' is used to describe a non-hierarchical mode of movement and branching, horizontal rather than vertical, and able to grow from any point. What Deleuze suggests is a structure without beginning or end, origin or destination (263).

With the Greek meaning of 'rhizome' being 'rootstalk', Deleuze and Guattari, applying this image to words, assert that words have 'multiple roots', and find that 'Joyce's words accurately shatter the linearity of words, even of language' (6), for 'a semiotic chain is like a tuber agglomerating very diverse acts, not only linguistic, but also perceptive, mimetic, gestural, and cognitive' (7). Although they do not include Woolf in their discussion of the 'roots' of words, her discussion of 'words' in 'Craftsmanship' certainly reflects their stance, and her use of the word 'root' and words that relate to it clearly undermines any singular root or origin. Language, for Deleuze and Guattari, 'stabilizes around a parish, a bishopric, a capital. It forms a bulb. It evolves by subterranean stems and flows, along river valleys or train tracks; it spreads like a patch of oil' (7). What Deleuze suggests is a structure 'without beginning or end, origin or destination; it is always in the middle (290). And in speaking about Woolf, Deleuze and Guattari talk about 'becomings' – 'to be between, to pass between, the intermezzo – that is what Virginia Woolf lived with all her energies, in all her work, never ceasing to become' (277). Deleuze and Guattari's description resonates with the movement, the energy and the open destinations of the 'essayistic'.

The word 'root', used by Woolf and suggestive of origin, etymology, stability, stasis, home, ground, ancestry and anchorage, is indicative of place and a certain lack of mobility; simultaneously, in some contexts, roots serve to transport nourishment, store food, and with growth, ironically, to encompass movement – but this movement is downward, while 'above is embryonic skin' (6). Clearly, roots – or words that resonate with rootedness, with the location of roots – exhibit differing contextual meanings for readers as they navigate the corpus of Woolf's writings. It also looks back to Montaigne, who found that 'forms of speech, like plants, improve and grow stronger by being transplanted' (III:5, 665). Why are there so many differing uses and functions for these references to being 'rooted', 'planted', stationary or fixed, and why her comments in her early diary that 'every hamlet, I doubt not, has its tiny roots deep twisted into the main root of the land'? And why later, in that diary, is there the suggestion of constraint by being imprisoned by roots, for 'our modern house . . . is planted deep in the ground', as she compares it to 'a prison' (*PA* 208). One also questions why there are so many references in Woolf's writings to flowers tugging at their roots, as if trying to free themselves – to '[cutting] roots with a penknife' (*VO* 33), or in *Jacob's Room,* to tearing 'the grass short at the roots' (29), or the frustration implicit in watching as 'the corn squirms and abases itself as if preparing to tug itself free from the roots, and yet is tied down' (104). What is signified by the multitude of references to constraints by 'roots' – of being imprisoned, tied down, cutting them with a knife to free oneself, or having one's feet 'planted', or 'a chair's legs planted in the bowels of the earth' (*VO* 293)?

Looking back to 'roots' and links with the land in *A Room of One's Own*, we have yet another mythic context, for here 'the swine rootled,' and pigs have links to Demeter, with both pigs and women sacrificed, so the land will be fertilised with blood (Harrison 125).[6] With Demeter, the goddess of pigs, and Rachel, referred to as 'a jolly little pig' (178–9), one who later sees 'a woman slicing a man's head off with a knife' (395) in a reversal of the Medusa, one finds the mythological significance of pigs, to links with the earth, with regenerative powers; and so one is not surprised to find Rachel 'walking faster and faster, her body trying to outrun her mind . . . as she sank down into the earth' (175), or to her ultimate death, in the light of the Greek myths about women. There is an ambivalence in Rachel regarding the sense of being rooted, being free, as revealed by the body/mind struggles. Interestingly, one of the roots of the word 'wild', the Latin *ferus*, or iron, suggests the antithesis of the many pages of definitions in the *OED*. It appears as an image of a 'hand dropped abrupt as iron on Rachel's shoulder' and 'she fell beneath it, and the grass whipped across her eyes and filled her mouth and ears' (*VO* 283). Here the grass, linked with Rachel, functions to eliminate the senses, as the eyes and ears are covered, and her voice gone.

The rooting relates to Jinny, in *The Waves*, who states: 'I am rooted but I flow . . . and like a limpet, I am broken off' (*W* 246), as she describes a sexual encounter. The tension in this opposition has great energy. This struggle with roots, with origins, with anchorage is suggested by the contradictory status of the metaphors. While Woolf was writing *To the Lighthouse*, her diary reveals an important connection between the mind and the grass: 'the talk by machinery does not charm, or suggest: it cuts the grass of the mind close to the roots' (*DIII*, 3 February 1927). The 'talk by machinery' conjures up a polished, fixed language that, like the manicured lawns, cuts the grass smoothly, right to the roots. When referencing other support structures, like 'scaffolding', Woolf's diary entry of 26 January 1920 relates her 'new form for a new novel', for it has 'no scaffolding, scarcely a brick to be seen; all crepuscular, but the heart, the passion, humour, everything as bright as fire in the mist' (*DII* 13–14). She seems to want to rid herself of a certain kind of anchorage, of rigid foundations, looking toward something new and filled with increasingly fluid qualities.

The idea of questioning foundations, of looking into these support structures, is often used by Woolf, along with her many references to structures like 'pavements' that cover, crush, conceal or replace plants – life. In David Bradshaw's discussion of the condemnation of militarism and war in Woolf's *Mrs Dalloway*,[7] focusing on 'the memorial moment and the monumental features', as well as Woolf's treatment of 'the boy soldiers' in the reserve army, 'the Territorial Army', one finds an earlier use of Woolf's metaphor of the laying of 'pavement', this time in relation to the 'monuments' and other edifices of England. In this case, at Finsbury Pavement, the place where a wreath is to be placed against the Cenotaph by young soldiers walking up Whitehall,

Bradshaw examines Peter Walsh's response as the 'boys in uniform carrying guns . . . marched, their arms stiff, and on their faces an expression like the letters of a legend written round the base of the statue praising duty, gratitude, fidelity, love of England' (43). Here, Bradshaw finds that 'Walsh, too, has been militarized, and recruited' for it was, 'in their steady way, as if *one will* worked legs and arms uniformly, and life, with its varieties, its irreticences, had been laid under a pavement of monuments and wreaths and drugged into a stiff yet staring corpse by discipline' (44; emphasis added by Bradshaw). The smooth, stiff and orderly state of this scene, with its stone monument, has links with the buildings Woolf's narrator leans against in *A Room of One's Own*, and like the paving over of the wild grasses at Oxbridge, now we have once again paved over 'life, with its varieties, its irreticences'.[8]

One of the most intriguing aspects of investigating Woolf's use of the words 'wild', 'grass', and so often, 'wild grass', is their frequent links – in varying contexts – with the freedom and adventures desired for young girls and women. Why is there this reverberation of the 'wild' in all of her writings? Examples include 'wild spirits' in *Books and Portraits*, the 'wildest scribble of contradictory jottings' in *A Room of One's Own*, the 'wild utterances' in 'On Not Knowing Greek' (*CRI* 29), the 'wild books' from 'Street Haunting' (*DM* 29), and, of course, Mrs. Ramsey, looking to the lighthouse: 'the green sand dunes with wild flowing grasses on them, which always seemed to be running away into some moon country, uninhabited of men' (*TL* 17). In my original inquiry into 'wildness', I utilised Hayden White's *Tropics of Discourse*; here he examines the survival of the word 'wildness' in its dialectical relation to 'civilisation'. Tracing the notion of the Wild Man from biblical times to the present, he associates the wilderness – desert, forest, jungle and mountains – with parts of the physical world not yet domesticated. As these wildernesses were brought under control, the idea of the Wild Man was transformed and internalised. Now modern cultural anthropology has conceptualised the idea of wildness as the repressed content of both civilised and primitive humanity. So instead of the relatively comforting thought that the Wild Man may exist out there and can be contained by some kind of physical action, it is now thought that this wildness is lurking within, and perhaps clamouring for release. At the same time, the idea of the wild woman as seductress began to merge with medieval notions of the demon, the devil and the witch, and she, above all, had to be contained (see White 165–73).

Woolf, in her writings, seems to have appropriated the word 'wild' to redefine it, repossess it, and reinvent it as a strongly positive mode of being for women – a mode of resistance. Perhaps re-appropriation is a more accurate characterisation of the linkage of women with the wild, for our early goddesses were very powerful and our myths also exemplify the fear of this power – the need to decapitate Medusa in order to avoid being turned to stone by her gaze. But, for Linden Peach, Woolf is 'reclaiming our innate sense of strangeness' (Peach 101), a sense of the foreign – or perhaps the savage – that resides within.

Analysing 'the mixed treatment of foreignness' in Woolf's work, Helen Southworth's exploration of the qualities of nostalgia, rootedness and foreignness in *Orlando* resonates with the 'wildness' and homelessness addressed in Woolf's other writings. Southworth finds in Orlando's response to Constantinople 'a landscape as antithetical to home' and points to 'the pleasure that he, as one who is English to the core, takes in this new landscape' (116).[9] The narrator relates how Orlando, 'who was English root and fibre, should yet exult to the depths of his heart in this wild panorama' (O 121). Upon going home, however, Southworth draws attention to 'an English landscape that erupts in the bald [Turkish] mountainside' (O 150). Reminiscent of *The Voyage Out*, where England was viewed by the travellers within the 'foreign' landscape, Orlando finds 'a great park-like space opened in the flank of the hill. Within, she could see an undulating and grassy lawn; she could see Oak trees dotted here and . . . a summer's day in England' (O 150–1). The return home for Orlando, which also resonates with a loss of the 'wildness' and freedom of the experience of South America in *The Voyage Out*, now 'meant conventionality, meant slavery . . . and restraining her tongue' (O 163). The inequity of gender roles was apparent to Orlando, as she thought of pouring tea in London.

This loss of freedom, the constraints of ceremony and convention, the slavery, the limitations, the inequities, providing the 'peace of mind' found in the courts and quadrangles of Oxbridge and in London, is, however, not to be found in the places of the 'other'. For Hayden White, 'it was the oppressed, exploited, alienated, or repressed part of humanity that kept on reappearing in the imagination of Western man . . . sometimes as a threat, and a nightmare, at other times as a goal and a dream . . . but always as a criticism of whatever security and peace of mind one group of men in society had purchased at the cost of the suffering of another' (White 180). And so the word 'peace', expressed as the 'security and peace of mind' that many in our culture possess, is also reinterpreted, reconstituted – by the so-called 'civilised' and 'uncivilised' – for their own needs.

Investigating the concepts of 'wildness' and 'civilisation', I re-read these passages through the lens of Montaigne's 'Of Cannibals', an essay Woolf knew quite well. There Montaigne observes that 'each man calls barbarism whatever is not his own practice.' Although the savages described can be considered 'barbarian', he feels that 'we surpass them in every kind of barbarity' (I:31, 152–3). Montaigne wants his readers to 'identify the artificiality in themselves, to recognize the extent to which their superficial civilization masks a deeper barbarism'. He wants, as Woolf does, to give his readers some critical distance on the nature of their so-called 'civilised' lives – to think about the vices of the 'civilised'. In 'Of Cannibals', Montaigne's 'encounter with cultural otherness is useful in understanding the colonialism that was in place when he was writing, and in approaching the colonialism in place during Woolf's lifetime and, of course, our own. Dudley Marchi's exploration of this aspect of Montaigne's writings is essential in relation to reading Woolf's texts – especially the colonial aspects in *The Voyage Out* – and since colonialism played so great a part in the context of her life in England. Montaigne had information on the French experience in the coastal regions of Brazil during the 1550s and knew of 'the anthropophagy of the Tupinamba'[10]; he read about them through Léry[11] and compared them with the European colonisers. The 'barbaric' in Montaigne's usage assumes 'an extremely mutable identity'; the term 'barbare', for Montaigne, 'has shifted to take on the positive sense of being 'uncorrupted' (Marchi 40), but Montaigne 'gives us an array of shifting terms, values, and criteria in which his judgement (and ours) is caught up in the perpetual instability of language and interpretation' (43). According to Marchi, Montaigne 'challenges his readers to consider the problematic of cultural relativism by claiming that the Europeans are truly "barbares" (cruel and brutal), as demonstrated by the atrocities committed during the religious wars, or by the examples of the colonialist savagery as alluded to in "*Des Cannibales*" and more fully in "*Des Coches*"' (Marchi 46). Montaigne's views on New World cannibals were quite different from what Europe had imagined them to be. Since he had met some Tupinamba at Rouen in 1563, he found their 'candid judgments of French society' (43) extremely revealing.

In his essay, 'Of Coaches', Montaigne also writes about the Mayan and Aztec cultures. In describing these people fighting for their liberty 'rather than submit to the domination of those by whom they had been so shamefully deceived', he speaks of how 'we took advantage of their ignorance and inexperience to incline them the more easily toward treachery, lewdness, avarice, and every sort of inhumanity and cruelty,' and tells his readers of 'so many cities razed, so many nations exterminated, so many millions of people put to the sword with the richest and most beautiful part of the world turned upside down for the traffic in pearls and pepper!' Woolf quotes from 'Of Coaches' in her essay,

'Montaigne' (III:6, 695), as she adds Montaigne's strong indictment of colonialism. Clearly her readings of Montaigne, of his experience of colonialism in the late sixteenth century, and her familiarity with the British Empire, had great impact on *The Voyage Out* and her dealings with the place of the 'other'.

Looking at the 'smooth lawns' in all their artifice, their very civilised, orderly and controlled being, and the 'wild grasses', the natural, untamed, passionate being in the context of Montaigne's 'Of Cannibals', one finds a similar dynamic. For Woolf, the 'civilisation' of the smooth lawns contains within it the 'barbarism' they have masked. It has simply been paved over, hidden from view, from consciousness. On the other hand, the 'wild grasses', with their passion and vitality, have the potential to create something better and must not allow subjugation. Implicit in these wild grasses is a resistance – with no trimming, cutting or levelling, no regulation. As Rachel Bowlby suggests: 'Women's exclusion from access to the means of being "trained"' offers a means of resistance, and the maintenance of 'the wandering, cartwheeling mind' (37–8), and those 'wild grasses' echo that resistance. It also involves the refusal of the machinery to regulate and control. And so for Woolf, the 'wild' and the 'primitive – looked upon by the so-called 'civilised' with fear, disgust and rage – are given positive valences.

Many questions surrounding Woolf's utilisation of the primitive have been assessed by Tuzyline Allan, and here she clearly establishes Woolf's double status – one that is 'both inside and outside of her civilization'. Allan, echoing Adrienne Rich's oft-quoted phrase, finds Woolf 'disloyal to civilization'. She elaborates on the plethora of myths about Africa in Woolf's England, which weighed heavily against the African subject; and, since national identity is far from stable, she poses important questions, in this wonderfully nuanced discussion, about Woolf's narration of the English nation, and about how Woolf's narrator describes the landscape in the travels in *The Voyage Out*. She finds similarities between the language of the very early European travellers which captured Africa's enchanting beauty, and Woolf's descriptions of the landscape in *The Voyage Out*. She cites the 'mantra of resistance' from *Three Guineas*, one that sounds so loudly, even in silence: 'As a woman I have no country. As a woman I want no country. As a woman my country is the whole world' (109). 'This eruption of what might be called 'bound-less desire', Allan suggests, 'is a post-colonial act that bears prophetic witness to the imminent demise of Empire and prefigures the trans-nationalism of post-imperial society' (118). In Allan's discussion of Norbert Elias's *The Civilizing Process,* she explores the extremely complicated nature of any attempt to define 'civilised' and 'uncivilised' in today's world, given 'Europe's colonial expansion' (121).[12] This complicated issue certainly comes across in Woolf's use of 'wild', aligned as it is with the 'savage', the 'barbaric' and the 'other'.

Those in the role of prostitutes are also outside, and they also encode and enact a certain 'wildness' in so many of Woolf's works. Celia Marshik, in her study of prostitution and censorship, points out that Woolf used prostitutes to interrogate the ideological organisation of social space that forcibly domesticated many middle-class women. Prostitutes are, in British idiom, 'public women'; hence they are part of the 'wild', the 'undomesticated', the definitely 'uncivilised' of British culture. The social purity movements,[13] policing both textual and sexual bodies, felt the need to clean up the public sphere. For Woolf, as Marshik notes, the social purity people had 'discreditable desires under the disguise of loving their kind' (860). Their fear of unchaste women polluting their environment was palpable. 'Public women' – prostitutes – were depicted as foreign agents, infecting 'civilisation'. For Rachel, the prostitutes of Piccadilly are 'terrifying and disgusting'. Domestication – opposed to the 'wild' – is enforced in Rachel's world. In *The Voyage Out*, as Marshik notes, Helen places the businessman on a continuum with the prostitute. Both are engaged in trade but, according to Helen, 'Thornbury is by far the worse whore' (863). Helen defends the prostitute while exposing the inhumanity of the English tourists. The English tourists felt themselves to be 'tight-coated soldiers among the soft instinctive people' (*VO* 285). In *Between the Acts* one finds another figure considered a 'loose woman' and, as Evelyn Haller[14] points out, Mrs. Manresa – who 'makes the grass tremble' – is referred to as 'wild child' seven times in the text; she is also described as a 'goddess, buoyant, abundant . . . an admirable woman, all sensation' (202).

Woolf's references to prostitutes in so many of her works conjures up links to wildness, to passion, to lack of control, to a life outside of society – outside of 'civilised' society – but one in which these women are also enslaved and commodified by that society. But how do we differentiate those women in Woolf's texts – the ones chased by the Beadle, excluded from the library, from education, the ones with the desire to transcend their culturally determined destiny, and their potential for 'wildness – from the other 'wild' women with the 'crimson nails' who enact their enslavement more explicitly?

Woolf's attempt to envision a transformed world, one in which she will no longer question what constitutes 'her' civilisation, certainly begins with her own awareness, with her struggle not be hypnotised, as she advocates in *Three Guineas*; and her thoughts are about a new kind of 'peace' that does not equate with lifelessness, clearly not the kind of peace that prevails when one must 'stay on the paths' of her culture's esteemed institutions. Woolf's desire to change the rules is evident in the politics of her writing, in the politics of her language. And this resistance to the regimentation of others, to the purification by others, is, as noted earlier, present in Woolf's essay, 'Craftsmanship', for here we are informed that words are much less bound by ceremony and convention than we are, and indeed, 'the less we enquire into the past of our dear Mother English', the better it will be for that lady's reputation: 'For she has gone a-roving, a roving fair maid' (205). It is also confirmed in Woolf's essay, 'Montaigne': 'The laws are mere conventions, utterly unable to keep touch with the vast variety and turmoil of human impulses; habits and customs are a convenience devised for the support of timid natures who dare not allow their souls free play' (*CRI* 67).

Looking to the *London Scene* essays, one finds, as Pamela Caughie suggests, significant connections between the 'controlled activity of the docks and the wild confusion of Oxford Street', the 'severely utilitarian' temper of the docks and the 'garishness and gaudiness' – the 'wildness' – of Oxford Street. Here, according to Caughie, Woolf 'tests out the complex relationship between writing styles and material circumstances' (Caughie 119–20). Dock Street deals with measurable substances, is dismal, forlorn, anchored; Oxford Street is flowing, has style, is glittery, bright and a breeding ground of sensation. As Caughie points out, 'The strength of Woolf's writing is its refusal to simplify and its awareness of its own relation to the signifying systems it exposes. It refuses to be anchored to the docks of London but flows with the tide of Oxford Street' (137).

I will end with 'Street Haunting', for here, within the complexity of this essay, Woolf interrogates the complexity of 'civilisation':

> The good citizen when he opens his door in the evening must be banker, golfer, husband, father; not a nomad wandering the desert, a mystic staring at the sky, a debauchee in the slums of San Francisco, a soldier heading a revolution, a pariah howling with scepticism and solitude. (*DM* 29)

One needs 'these thwarting currents of being; here we balance ourselves after the splendours and miseries of the streets. . . . Second-hand books are wild books, homeless books; they have come together in vast flocks of variegated feather, and have a charm which the domesticated volumes of the library lack' (29). The 'wild', the undomesticated, need to resist so-called 'civilisation', the ceremony, the conventions, the oppressive life, the silencing, the colonial exploitation, the 'official story'. They will create something new and different, and perhaps more than a little wild. And the women of the twenty-first century must continue to heed Woolf's advice.

Notes

1. Virginia Woolf ([1929] 1957), *A Room of One's Own* (New York, NY: Harcourt Brace Jovanovich).
2. See Martha Vicinus (1972), *Suffer and Be Still* (Bloomington, IN: Indiana University Press).
3. See Roger Celestin (1996), *From Cannibals to Radical: Figures and Limits of Exoticism* (Minneapolis, MN: University of Minnesota Press), 32. Celestin finds Montaigne's 'Of Coaches' an anti-colonialist indictment.
4. Virginia Woolf [1927] (1955), *To the Lighthouse*, Harcourt Brace.
5. Gilles Deleuze and Félix Guattari (1987), *A Thousand Plateaus: Capitalism and Schizophrenia*, trans. and foreword Brian Massumi (Minneapolis, MN: University of Minnesota Press).
6. See Jane Harrison ([1903] 1991), *Prolegomena to the Study of Greek Religion*, 3rd edn, Princeton, NJ: Princeton University Press.
7. David Bradshaw (2002), '"Vanished Like Leaves": The Military, Elegy and Italy in *Mrs Dalloway*', *WSA* 8, 111.
8. 'Irreticences' is a word Woolf made up; it means outspokenness, the act of speaking freely, and lack of restraint. It is no surprise that she would create a word with meanings that express her greatest desires for herself. See Regina Fowler (2002), 'Virginia Woolf: Lexicographer', *English Language Notes* 39, 61.
9. Southworth, Helen (2005), '"Mixed Virginia": Reconciling the "Stigma of Nationality" and the Sting of Nostalgia in Virginia Woolf's Later Fiction', *Woolf Studies Annual* 11, 99–132. See Southworth's article (2007), 'Virginia Woolf's "Wild England": and George Borrow, Autoethnography, and *Between the Acts*', *Studies in the Novel* 39(2) (Summer), 196–215, in which 'homelessness and vagabondage are central figures' (198).
10. The Tupinamba were a tribe in Brazil colonised by the Portuguese in the sixteenth century; Montaigne read about them, wrote about them, and met them in Paris. He writes about colonialism in 'Of Cannibals' and 'Of Coaches', describing in the latter the horrific things that were done to the colonised. Of course, Woolf read these accounts in the *Essays*. See Dudley Marchi (1993), 'Montaigne and the New World', *Modern Language Studies* 23(4) (Autumn), 35–54.
11. Jean de Léry, a missionary who studied the New World in his work (1975), *Histoire d'un voyage fait en la terre du Brésil* (Geneva: Droz). According to Dudley Marchi, 'this work provided Montaigne with the greater part of his information on the French experience with the coastal regions of Brazil in the 1550s.' See Marchi's work in note 10.
12. Tuzyline Allan's eloquent article (1999), 'Civilisation, Its Pretexts, and Virginia Woolf's Imagination', collected in *Virginia Woolf and Communities*, provokes many new questions regarding Woolf and the subject of post-colonialism.
13. The social purity movement of the late nineteenth century sought to abolish prostitution and other sexual activities that its members thought immoral. See Celia Marshik (1999), 'Publication and "Public Women": Prostitution

and Censorship in Three Novels by Virginia Woolf', *MFS* 45(4) (Winter), 853–86.

14. Evelyn Haller (1992), 'Virginia Woolf and Katherine Mansfield: Or, the Case of the Déclassé Wild Child', *Virginia Woolf Miscellanies*, ed. Mark Hussey and Vara Neverow-Turk, 96–104.

Part III

Dialogue and Dissent

Chapter 5

Thinking and Talking/War and Peace

The Germans were over this house last night and the night before that. Here they are again. It is a queer experience lying in the dark and listening to the zoom of a hornet which may at any moment sting you to death.
Virginia Woolf, 'Thoughts on Peace in an Air Raid'[1]

These are terrifying words, and certainly gain the reader's attention. My epigraph is the opening of Woolf's 1940 essay, 'Thoughts on Peace in an Air Raid', conveying the voice of a witness to these bombings. From Woolf's letters and diary entries, we know that she was a witness, and suffered as witnesses of atrocities suffer. The immediate focus is sound, for 'it is a sound that interrupts cool and consecutive thinking about peace. Yet it is a sound – far more than prayers or anthems – that should compel one to think about peace' (*DM* 243). It is always difficult to read Woolf's letters and diary entries from this period, for she talks of people who were killed by 'bombs' and 'landmines', and uses the word 'terror' in relation to the bombing; in relation to the war in Spain, she speaks of the 'photographs of dead bodies and ruined houses', the ones that she uses as a refrain (without photographs) in *Three Guineas* (1938). These words of war made up the lexicon of Woolf's life in the early twentieth century, but this war-time essay sends out a call for a different kind of language, some new ways of communicating or even negotiating – as words become the new weaponry.

Those potential 'weapons', those different kinds of conversation, are talked about, but first we hear the words of a young man sent to fight:

To fight against a real enemy, to earn undying honour and glory by shooting total strangers, and to come home with my breast covered with medals and decorations, that was the summit of my hope. . . . It was for this that my whole life so far had been dedicated, my education, training, everything. (246)

Quoting the words of a soldier from the last war, a question about 'Disarmament' arises, and doubts about its effectiveness follow. Perhaps 'writing "Disarmament" on a sheet of paper at a conference table' will not be enough. Woolf knew Arthur Ponsonby, a Member of Parliament, quite well, and was probably familiar with his speech, 'Disarmament by Example',[2] presented in the House of Commons on 17 March 1927. Published by the No More War Movement, it sold for 1 penny. In George Lansbury's Foreword, he notes the lack of 'sneers and jokes', for the ministers 'were obliged to treat the whole discussion in the most serious manner' (2). Interestingly, given the recent US decision to deploy 30,000 troops to Afghanistan, Ponsonby was moving to reduce the Air Force by 33,000 men (3). In speaking of his recent trip to America, Ponsonby was struck by 'the vast foreign populations . . . living together, mingling together, in amity, in unity, in cooperation, without any difficulty at all. Why? Because they have not got governments to egg them on one against the other' (8). His opinion of America in the 1920s – between the major wars – seems quite idealistic today. And yet his idea of every nation making the decision to disarm would surely be followed by many others, for 'disarmament by example must be popularized as the new road' (11). It was not enough.

The response to the question about writing the word 'Disarmament' on a sheet of paper shows its limitations as the sole solution, for the narrator reminds the readers that 'Othello's occupation will be gone, but he will remain Othello': 'The young airman up in the sky is driven not only by the voices of loudspeakers; he is driven by voices within himself – ancient instincts, instincts fostered and cherished by education and tradition' (*DM* 246). As we look at 'disarmament' today, at 'nuclear nonproliferation treaties', at Daniel Ellsberg's recent reports on what went on during the bombing of Hiroshima and Nagasaki, at 'unmanned drones' that eliminate the need for so many soldiers on the ground, and the definitions of 'civilian', 'noncombatant', 'contractor', 'surgical strikes', 'cluster bombs' and 'clean bombs', we ask how much control we have in a 'democracy' to weigh in on these matters regarding 'wars' that are no longer officially declared. What have we gained as we continue on the old road, not the 'new road' Ponsonby talked about in 1927?

Much has been written in response to the attacks of 9/11, and more is being written in criticism of some of those responses. Here is an excerpt from Susan Sontag's[3] response in *The New Yorker* of 24 September 2001:

> The voices licensed to follow the event seem to have joined together in a campaign to infantilize the public. Where is the acknowledgement that this was not a 'cowardly' attack on 'civilization' or 'liberty' or 'humanity' or 'the free world' but an attack on the world's self-proclaimed super-power, undertaken as a consequence of specific American alliances and actions?

The negative responses filled the news media, and as Judith Butler notes in *Precarious Life*,[4] 'we have seen a rise in anti-intellectualism and a growing acceptance of censorship within the media' (Butler 1). Butler explores the responses to the question that was frequently asked after the beginning of the Afghanistan War: 'Why do they hate us so much?' The question was framed for very limited answers, and it took years – as I remember it – for a minimal degree of acceptance of anything other than those 'almost designated' answers. As Butler points out, 'the cry that "there is no excuse for September 11" has become a means by which to stifle any serious public discussion of how US foreign policy has helped to create a world in which such acts of terrorism are possible' (3). For Chalmers Johnson,[5] the term 'blowback', invented by the Central Intelligence Agency (CIA), refers to the unintended consequences of American policies, and his book of the same name, surprisingly published in 2000, is what we need to be concerned with as we escalate the war in Afghanistan, continue our drone raids on Pakistan, and take so many actions without informing the US citizenry. The 'torture memos' (see Mark Danner), extremely difficult to read, are the kinds of thing that governments want concealed, but good investigative reporting (see Jeremy Scahill, Mark Danner, and Glen Greenwald of Salon.com) matters for our democracies.

The kinds of conversation that need to take place, according to Butler, Arundhati Roy, Noam Chomsky, Dennis Kucinich and Barbara Lee, will allow questions that do not make it into the mainstream press, but are now available to those with computers; it means that libraries must have the Internet available, that there must be a library in your town, and that, once online, you have the ability to find reliable sources of 'information' and 'opinion'. We now have 'new media' – with blogs, Twitter, Facebook, e-mail and texting – with the potential for significant 'information' to be gained and 'interactions' to take place, those conversations and debates so necessary for a thriving democracy. In *Blogging*, Jill Walker Rettberg explores the changes that many see in the decline of the public sphere, a concept introduced by Jurgen Habermas.[6] The ideal public space, to many that have concerns about the isolation of the public, has now been transformed, in the minds of many, by technology. Richard Sennett,[7] in 1986, before the Internet was in almost every household, blamed the demise of the public sphere on radio and television, and on a lack of interaction. With Woolf's call for a participatory audience, it is interesting that Bertolt Brecht,[8] 'who aimed at creating theatre that would make people think critically rather than simply sit back and be entertained, wrote about the potential for a different kind of radio in 1932' (Rettberg 53). Brecht wanted a two-way radio for the purpose of communication, and apparently that was what the original radio was like; it later became a mass medium, the broadcast being presented to a passive audience. Brecht wanted radio 'to give a truly public character to public occasions', but this was not possible (Rettberg 53).

For Virginia Woolf, the conversational mode offered a way to engage her readers while simultaneously avoiding an authoritative stance in her writings. She experimented with dialogue in her 1920 and 1923 essays, 'A Talk About Memoirs' and 'Mr. Conrad: A Conversation' (*EIII* 180, 376), and it finds its way, in ever-increasing complexity, into many essays: 'Montaigne', *A Room of One's Own*, 'On Not Knowing Greek', 'How Should One Read a Book?', *Three Guineas* and 'Thoughts on Peace in an Air Raid'. These essays enact an intricate dialogic involving a multitude of voices that enable Woolf's narrators – in their interactions with these voices – to display many contradictory perspectives. Her narrators engage in a performance that functions to unsettle and awaken her readers, and, in a Brechtian sense, to 'defamiliarise' cultural institutions heretofore accepted as 'natural' but which are simply constructs.[9] This chapter will focus on Woolf's 1940 essay, 'Thoughts on Peace in an Air Raid', as it interrogates and responds to the fascism so pervasive in both the public and private spheres of her life. Through the lens of both Michel de Montaigne and Mikhail Bakhtin, I will explore Woolf's inclusion of varied voices, multiple conversations and conflicting viewpoints within this essay; ultimately, I will show the significance of the readers' struggles with these manifold voices – as they search for their own voices – in 1940s England and in today's ever so frightening world.

For Virginia Woolf, the 'essay' fights a battle similar to her own, for it also stands outside, resisting stasis and rigid definition, and takes its place beside women and other marginalised figures in order to critique the conventions and ceremonies of those in power. The essay's hybrid nature, its openness and freedom, all serve to resist the purity, totality and certainty of patriarchal/fascist modes of expression. The essay's crucial interaction with its readers – as well as the many conversations embedded within it – serves to perpetuate the indeterminacy of its potential meanings. This aspect of the essay is not surprising given its origins in letters and dialogues. Montaigne also fills his essays with other voices, with quotations – re-contextualising them within his essays – offering conflicting ideas and thus not making judgements for his readers. In Woolf's 'How Should One Read a Book?', her narrator advises that readers 'take no advice' and 'to follow your own instincts . . .' (258).

Conversations do not simply resist an authoritarian stance, but function to move readers in a multitude of directions, expose them to differing perspectives and, using Montaigne's tennis analogy, place the ball in their court. But what if the ball goes astray? What if the questions asked have been programmed to exclude certain answers? How is everything being framed? The reader's task is increasingly difficult but more rewarding. Bakhtin comments on authoritative discourse, and sounds very much like Woolf as he speaks of 'its inertia, its semantic finiteness, its calcification' (*DI* 343); in 'Craftsmanship', Woolf's narrator conjures up the death of words if we 'pin words down to one meaning', for 'they hate anything that stamps them with one meaning' (*DM* 206). The actual struggle with the language and ideas of others – the conversation – is significant. Bakhtin calls attention to 'the importance of struggling with the discourse of others', and explores 'its influence in the history of an individual's coming to ideological consciousness' (*DI* 348).

This is evident in the dialogic aspect of the Montaignean essay and, I will argue, the Woolfian essay, for both insist on a diversity of voices and create a situation not unlike our everyday discourse with others; we are, after all, always assessing the language of others, their tone of voice, and our own expectations. As Bakhtin asserts:

> We can go so far as to say that in real life people talk most of all about what others talk about – they transmit, recall, weigh, and pass judgment on other people's words, opinions, assertions, information; people are upset by others' words, or agree with them, contest them . . . At every step one meets a 'quotation' or a 'reference' to something that a particular person said . . . to one's own previous words, to a newspaper. . . . Thus talk goes on about speaking people and their words everywhere. (*DI* 338–9)

The problematic nature of these activities – interpreting and quoting other voices – was also conveyed by Montaigne to his readers in the 1580s:

> It is more of a job to interpret the interpretations than to interpret the things, and there are more books about books than about any other subject: we do nothing but write glosses about each other. The world is swarming with commentaries; of authors there is great scarcity. (III:13, 818)

Both Montaigne and Woolf struggle with other voices – as their readers struggle – to find new modes of expression, to find their own voice. 'Thoughts on Peace in an Air Raid' clearly presents this challenge to its readers.

Woolf includes a multitude of voices in 'Thoughts on Peace' – narrators, quotations from loudspeakers and politicians, William Blake, Sir Thomas Browne, newspapers, radio, Lady Astor and a young Englishman who fought in the last war; additionally, her narrator calls attention to those internalised voices within the young airman now up in the sky. Driven by those voices within himself – 'ancient instincts, instincts fostered and cherished by education and tradition' (246) – these voices are also clearly internalised and echoed by the women in this text. Woolf's thinking about the issue of instinct during this period – at a time when she was reading several of Freud's works[10] – is expressed in her diary entry of 9 December 1939: 'If we're all instinct, the unconscious, what's all this about civilization, the whole man, freedom, &c?' (*DV* 250). In her letter to Shena, Lady Simon, on 22 January 1940, Woolf asks questions about 'removing men's disabilities' and whether we can 'change sex characteristics?'. She also asks whether 'the women's movement [is] a remarkable experiment in that transformation? Mustn't our next task be the emancipation of man? How can we alter the crest and spur of the fighting cock?' (*LVI* 379). Questioning the responsibility for war – while taking responsibility for transforming men's attitudes towards war – Woolf's narrator foregrounds the binary thinking of that time; men had responsibility for war, and women were responsible for peace.

According to Woolf's diary entries, the air raid warnings began in September 1939, and by August 1940, the time Woolf was writing this essay, she wrote in her diary: 'Yesterday . . . there was a roar. Right on top of us they came. I looked at the plane, like a minnow at a roaring shark' (*D5* 312). 'Now we are in the war. England is being attacked. I got this feeling for the first time yesterday. The feeling of pressure, danger, horror' (*DV* 313). 'A bomb dropped so close I cursed Leonard for slamming the window.' 'I try to imagine how one's killed by a bomb. I've got it fairly vivid – the sensation: but cant [sic] see anything but suffocating nonentity following after' (*DV* 326). 'Thoughts on Peace', like these diary entries, evokes the horrifying sounds of war, sounds that interrupt 'thinking about peace':

> The Germans were over this house last night and the night before that. Here they are again. It is a queer experience, lying in the dark and listening to the zoom of a hornet, which may at any moment sting you to death. It is a sound that interrupts cool and consecutive thinking about peace. Yet it is a sound – far more than prayers and anthems – that should compel one to think about peace. (*DM* 243)

In a letter to Shena, Lady Simon, Woolf reflects on writing 'Thoughts on Peace': 'what the Americans want of me is views on peace – well these spring from views on war' (*LVI* 379). As Woolf's title indicates, 'peace' is spoken of in the context of 'war', of 'bombing', for they are inseparable. Given the polarised view of gender at the time, women would be expected to limit their writings to 'peace'.

In preparation for writing 'Thoughts on Peace', Woolf recorded the following passage in her reading notebook of 1939–40: 'For now the male has also [. . .] his attributes in Hitler, & is fighting against them. Is this the first time a sex has turned against its own specific qualities? Compare with the woman [sic] movement' (Silver 116–17). Woolf also compiled a list of authors and phrases, and included the word 'cerebration', which translates as 'thinking' or simply refers to the mind or the brain. A significant diary entry on 15 May 1940 also finds its way into the essay: 'This idea struck me: the army is the body: I am the brain. Thinking is my fighting' (*DV* 285). Here Woolf links mind with body and equates thinking with fighting, thus transforming 'cerebration' into a weapon. These 'Reading Notes', along with Woolf's letters and diary entries from this period, raise many questions that permeate this essay – questions regarding the construction of gender, instinct versus reason and responsibility, and the power of language to transform our world. In 'Thoughts on Peace', Woolf utilises certain narrative and rhetorical strategies for the purpose of enabling her readers to revise their views, to see the complicity of those women within the text, and perhaps see their own complicity. Statements are made, questioned, qualified, sometimes re-qualified, and then restated in a new way. As readers, we also witness this complex process of thinking.

With the word 'cerebration' on her mind, Woolf's title announces her focus on 'thinking', as the narrator's use of 'we' and 'us' engage her readers in this process. The language is metaphoric, as the sounds of the 'hornet' and the 'saw' – the animate and inanimate that sting and cut – stand in for the sounds of planes carrying bombs. The zoom of the hornet moves to the mind as the sawing heard overhead moves to the brain. The weapon, the bomb, in the guise of the hornet and the saw, is being transferred to the mind or the brain, as the words 'think', 'mind', 'mental' and 'brain' pervade the text. The weapons, now part of the mind, have been transformed into language.

Edward Bishop has examined Woolf's use of metaphors in her essays to show how 'they are used deliberately to disturb the reader's unquestioned assumptions' and to involve those readers in Woolf's exploration of 'the complex relation between language, phenomenal reality, and thought' (Bishop, 'Metaphor', 573). The reader is made aware of 'the heuristic function of language', with 'words testing their connections with things' (579). As Bishop suggests, 'metaphor is by definition unsettling, effecting as it does a transfer from one realm to another' (579), as well as calling attention to language itself. The 'zoom of a hornet', a metaphor for the bomber overhead, interrupts thinking about peace. As the narrator waits for the bombs to drop in 'Thoughts on Peace', 'all thinking stopped' and 'all feeling, save one dull dread, ceased' (247). The emotions of fear and hate are linked to sterility and infertility, and only the demise of these emotions will bring the return of life, of creativity. Like the Beadle's interruption of her intellectual curiosity – the imaginings and the desires of one of the narrators in *A Room of One's Own* – the sterility and lack of fertility present here are expressed in terms of gender politics.

Patriarchy

With the fascists' conception of the strict polarisation of gender – the militaristic and the maternal – the construction of gender is a key question in this essay. Men are fighters and women are at home, weaponless. But these women have the potential to fight – if they 'fight with the mind' (244). Transferred from sky to mind, the hornet ends its journey as language, as words on the page of *The Times*, and these words, voiced by a woman writer, ironically express the following: 'Women have not a word to say in politics,' for 'all the idea-makers who are in a position to make ideas effective are men.' 'There are no women in the cabinet; nor in any *responsible* post' (244). The issue of women's responsibility is now foregrounded, for 'that is a thought that damps thinking and encourages *irresponsibility*' (my emphasis). 'Why not bury the head in the pillow, plug the ears, and cease this futile activity of idea-making?' Weapons and words have been connected, so for women to be weaponless is also to be without a voice, without a language for political purposes. The power to make change happen has been with men, but a woman's words on a page of *The Times*, in conversation with the narrator about 'responsible' government positions and the 'responsibility' of women to 'think' positively, may begin to undermine that singular power source.

The narrator, in dialogue with the woman's voice in *The Times*, explores the issue of women's resistance: 'Are we not stressing our disability because our ability exposes us perhaps to abuse, perhaps to contempt?' Calling for 'thinking against the current', thinking against the ideas put forth by loudspeakers and politicians, she risks contempt by calling attention to their propaganda: 'everyday they tell us that we are a free people, fighting to defend freedom' (244). Calling for women to 'puncture gas-bags and discover seeds of truth', she rejects their statement: 'It is not true that we are free,' for we are 'both prisoners' tonight – he 'boxed in his machine with a gun handy' and 'we lying in the dark with a gas mask handy' (245). Implicit in this pronouncement of their shared imprisonment is the state of denial in those who use the loudspeaker, and in those women who have been silently complicit with them. But she has broken that silence and others may follow.

The hornet entered the mind of a woman writing in *The Times*: 'Another sound begins sawing its way in the brain. "Women of ability" – it was Lady Astor speaking in *The Times* this morning – "are held down because of a subconscious Hitlerism in the hearts of men"' (245). The goal is to make the subconscious conscious, 'to drag [it] up into consciousness', for this Hitlerism is 'the desire for aggression; the desire to dominate and enslave' (245). The weapon is the process, the dredging up, the ability to expose these underlying feelings. What the narrator has exposed, has 'made visible', appears in the next few sentences; we are suddenly in the presence of prostitutes, of 'painted women: dressed-up women; women with crimson lips and crimson fingernails' (245). After 'showing' the enslavement, the narrator suggests that 'if we could free ourselves from slavery we should free men from tyranny. Hitlers are bred by slaves' (245). But separating the 'public' women from the 'domesticated' women, as noted above, does not change the fact that both are enslaved.

Let us return to the voice of a young Englishman who fought in the last war. The quotation of the young Englishman, referred to as 'another mind-hornet in the chambers of the brain', once again conveys what must be fought: 'To fight against a real enemy, to earn undying honour and glory by shooting total strangers, and to come home with my breast covered with medals and decorations, that was the summit of my hope. . . . It was for this that my whole life so far had been dedicated, my education, training, everything' (246).

This was not simply the hornet as weapon, as previously noted, but a combined 'mind-hornet', suggesting that the weapon is already part of the young Englishman's mind; this 'mind-hornet' is not simply the bomb, but represents – as his statement shows – the internalisation of certain ideas and values that constitute a very familiar construction of masculinity. Questions arise about his 'instincts' and how they relate to the maternal 'instinct'? Can we 'switch off the maternal instinct at the command of a table full of politicians?' (246). In 1941, Woolf again addressed this issue in a letter to Shena, Lady Simon: 'No, I dont [*sic*] see whats [*sic*] be done about war. Its manliness; and manliness breeds womanliness – both so hateful' (*LVI* 464).

Woolf's familiarity with fascists' writings on gender polarisation is evident in *Three Guineas*, as well as her Reading Notebooks. From her reading of Hilary Newitt's *Women Must Choose* (1937),[11] as well as the writings of Hitler and Mussolini, she found that war and maternity were frequently equated with one another. Hitler's 1934 speech, which Woolf would have found in Newitt, states: 'That which man sacrifices in the struggles of his people, woman sacrifices in the struggles to preserve the single cells of this people' (Newitt 40). Mussolini made similar statements regarding the 'nature' of men and women: 'War is to man what maternity is to the woman. I do not believe in perpetual peace; not only do I not believe in it, but I find it depressing' (Finer 175). Woolf's narrator attempts to deconstruct this so-called 'natural' division of the sexes as she mimics the words of the Englishman who loved fighting: 'The maternal instinct is a woman's glory. It was for this that my whole life has been dedicated, my education, training, everything' (247). Exposing the patriarchal desires that women have internalised and made their own, her narrator speaks – as the narrator of *Three Guineas* did – of the 'refusal to bear children', of 'other openings for [women's] creative power'. But most important at this point is the narrator's repetition of 'we must' in connection with women being responsible for freeing men of 'their fighting instinct', and bringing man 'out of his prison into the open air', for 'making happiness' and 'freeing him from the machine' (247). This action by women would seem to free the young Englishmen, until the narrator thinks of the young Germans and Italians who will remain slaves; and what do the women reading these words think of their own slavery? 'We must', in this context, must be stricken from women's vocabulary.

At this crucial point, another voice intrudes to join the interchange. Now we hear a captured enemy soldier speak of how happy he is that 'the fight is over!' The reader is shown an enemy soldier who hates fighting, takes tea with the families of his former enemies, and clearly desires peace; but the need to substitute something for 'the loss of his glory and his gun' is acknowledged. Freeing man from the machine may transform that sterility; now 'the seed may be fertile' (248). Bakhtin speaks of 'the alien voices that enter into the struggle for influence within an individual's consciousness' and says that 'a conversation with an internally persuasive word that one has begun to resist may continue, but it takes on another character: it is questioned . . . to expose its weak sides, to get a feel for its boundaries, to experience it physically as an object' (*DI* 348). Both men and women need to become aware of these 'alien voices' and need to be freed from their constrained roles, with men gaining 'access to creative feelings' and 'new openings for their creative power' (248, 247). But women are not solely responsible for that task. Woolf's complicated dialogic strategies are utilised to move her readers out of their complacency and complicity. In their struggle to find their own voices, readers become aware of opposing voices, and as Montaigne asserts: 'When someone opposes me, he arouses my attention, not my anger' (III:8, 705). The conversational mode is an awakening and enables critical thinking, 'thinking against the current'.

When Woolf's narrator speaks of 'other tables' beside 'the officer tables and conference tables' and the importance of 'thinking against the current', we can think of the very few today who are courageous enough to sit at those 'other' tables, to be that 'other', that 'outsider', to speak out, to resist, potentially to risk your life. And what if taking this action – in the equivocal words of Woolf's narrator – 'exposes us perhaps to abuse, perhaps to contempt'? Today we think of the country music group, the Dixie Chicks, and the blacklisting, death threats, and the burning of their CDs in response to their anti-Bush statements; Ayaan Hirsi Ali, the woman from Somalia who moved to the Netherlands and wrote a film called *Submission, Part I*, about defiance – about Muslim women who shift from total submission to God to a dialogue with their deity. Hirsi Ali remains under a death threat, but continues to speak out, with bodyguards in attendance. We look to the courage of Barbara Lee, the US Congresswoman from California and the only person in the entire US Congress to vote against funding the Afghanistan War in 2001. Finally, Brooksley Born, head of the Commodities Futures Trading Commission, not only warned of the potential economic meltdown in the late 1990s, but tried to convince key economic powerbrokers to take action that could have averted the 2008 world financial crisis.[12]

As we re-read 'Thoughts on Peace in an Air Raid' as the second decade of the twenty-first century begins, we still find a current that 'flows fast and furious' . . . 'in a spate of words from the loudspeakers and the politicians', that 'whirls a young airman up into the sky' (244). Today, we read about bombing deaths on a daily basis, in countries too numerous to mention, as we are bombarded with 'sound bites', strategic 'leaks' and fear-inspiring language from varied media outlets – unfortunately echoing the American government's political agenda. Efforts to constrain freedom, to stifle dissent, are fast becoming the norm. The necessary 'conversations' are silenced, propaganda once again winning the day. As we re-read Woolf today, we find that her comments on topics such as 'patriotism' and those 'prostituted fact-purveyors' – our newspapers – clearly resonate with the political situations we confront on a daily basis. This is a difficult essay to read at this time, but there is no more important time to read it once again – for the silencing of women's voices is still with us.

Notes

1. 'Thoughts on Peace in an Air Raid' ([1942] (1970)) is collected in *The Death of the Moth* (New York, NY: Harcourt Brace Jovanovich).
2. Arthur Ponsonby, friend of the Woolfs, fought hard for disarmament and spoke out against the problems of 'patriotism'. His pamphlet was published by the No More War Movement in 1927.

3. Susan Sontag was vilified for her comments soon after the attacks of 9/11. Others agreed with her but were afraid to take a public stance. One had to be viewed as 'patriotic' and she was seen as sympathetic to the terrorists. There was no middle ground.

4. Judith Butler's (2004) *Precarious Life: The Powers of Mourning and Violence* is an appraisal of the aftermath of 9/11, a critique of violence, and a search to find other ways to respond to current US policies which promote perpetual war.

5. Chalmers Johnson is known for his prescient work, *Blowback* (2000), and his other books, *The Sorrows of Empire* (2004) and *Nemesis* (1999).

6. Jurgen Habermas is best known for his work ([1962] (1991)), *The Structural Transformation of the Public Sphere: An Inquiry into a Category of Bourgeois Society*, Cambridge: Cambridge University Press, 46.

7. Richard Sennett (1986), *The Fall of Public Man*.

8. Bertolt Brecht ([1932] (1964)), 'The Radio as an Apparatus of Communication', in J. Willett (1967), *Brecht on Theatre*.

9. See J. Willett (1967), *Brecht on Theatre*, for 'alienation' techniques.

10. Hogarth Press published translations of Sigmund Freud's works from 1924 onwards. While writing 'Thoughts on Peace in an Air Raid', Woolf was reading several of his works, including *Moses and Monotheism* (1939) and *Civilisation, War and Death: Selections from Three Works by Sigmund Freud* (1939), ed. John Rickman, which included Freud's 1932 letter to Albert Einstein, 'Why War?', and *Group Psychology and the Analysis of the Ego* (1922).

11. Newitt's work documents the position of women under fascism in Germany, Italy and Austria, and exposes the careful training they underwent to make them an integral part of the machinery of the state. Hitler's 1934 speech, as quoted by Newitt, states: 'Man and woman must therefore mutually value and respect each other when they see that each performs the task which Nature and Providence have ordained' (*Women Must Choose*, 40–1).

12. In response to Brooksley Born's warning, and her calls for regulation of the secretive multi-million dollar derivatives market, Born was silenced and essentially dismissed by Alan Greenspan, Robert Rubin, and Larry Summers. See *Frontline*, 'The Warning', 20 October 2007 (PBS.org).

Chapter 6

Virginia Woolf, 'Patriotism', and 'our prostituted fact-purveyors'

Is it not possible that if we knew the truth about war, the glory of war would be scotched and crushed where it lies curled up in the rotten cabbage leaves of our prostituted fact-purveyors . . .?

Virginia Woolf, *Three Guineas*

Patriotism and its results – wars – give an enormous revenue to the newspaper trade, and profits to many other trades.

Leo Tolstoy, 'Patriotism and Government'

The narrowest patriotism could be made to appear noble, the foulest accusations could be represented as an indignant outburst of humanitarianism, and the meanest and most vindictive aims falsely disguised as idealism. Everything was legitimate which could make the soldiers go on fighting.

Arthur Ponsonby, *Falsehood in Wartime: Propaganda Lies of the First World War*

In her 1916 letter to Margaret Davies, Virginia Woolf expressed her feelings regarding World War I: 'I become steadily more feminist, owing to the *Times*, which I read at breakfast and wonder how this preposterous masculine fiction [the war] keeps going a day longer . . . Do you see any sense in it?' (*II2 76*). Woolf's question is still with us today, as we struggle, in this age of 'information', with our expanded media: newspapers, magazines, television, radio and Internet 'blog' sites. How did the United States – with major support from Great Britain – undertake this unfathomable pre-emptive war in Iraq? And if Woolf became 'steadily more feminist, owing to the *Times*', how have we been transformed by our news media's coverage of the Iraq War? As we re-read Virginia Woolf's *Three Guineas* in the twenty-first century, permeated as it is by repeated references to 'patriotism', 'prostituted fact-purveyors' and 'photographs of dead bodies and ruined houses', we are deeply saddened by the familiarity of it all – and outraged that this text is so very relevant to the state of our world today.

Investigating these uncanny connections, we are drawn to familiar words – 'patriotism', 'influence', 'opinion' and 'free' – words that Woolf's narrator explicitly foregrounds as 'words'; by placing them in varying contexts they are simply deprived of any definitive meaning. Described as 'used words', the narrator confirms that words like 'free' have come to 'mean so little' (153). It is interesting to note how a similar narrative strategy functions in *A Room of One's Own* concerning the repetition of the word 'opinion'. Here, Woolf's narrator resists defining this most provisional term and suggests: 'One can only show how one came to hold whatever opinion one does hold' (4). Recognising that 'what is amusing now . . . had to be taken in desperate earnest once' (57), the narrator acknowledges that our own perspectives, and the world's, always undergo change; they become 'opinions' which are transitory and contingent but are, nevertheless, inscribed as history. In *Three Guineas*, Woolf's narrator clearly undermines any distinction between the provisional 'opinion' and the clearly defined 'fact', for they have both been 'adulterated' (143) and are equally suspect. Together, in this particular context, many of these repetitive words – like 'influence' – will serve to interrogate and complicate one another as they contribute, in very different ways, to the effectiveness of the war effort. Propaganda, with its manipulation of language, its intentional distortion of 'facts' and its shaping of public opinion, ultimately ends with the well-known phrase coined by Walter Lippmann in his 1922 work, *Public Opinion*: 'the manufacturing of consent' (158). Woolf, in her narrative strategies, utilises the repetition of these significant words in order to manipulate language with a significantly different goal – that of 'manufacturing' a kind of critical thinking that will serve to undermine 'our prostituted fact-purveyors'. In the knowledge that some of our best newspapers and other media outlets have become 'our prostituted fact-purveyors' (*TG* 147), and our governments have become propaganda machines 'manufacturing consent', how can democracy function? And why, in 2009, do we still find those in power constantly repeating that dissent is 'unpatriotic', while those leaders of the opposition seem to cower in silence? There are, of course, informed people – critical thinkers – who continue to write exceptional letters of protest to their newspapers; these critical voices, the voices Woolf consistently calls forth, stand as the seeds of resistance, for they alone, in 2002, refused to accept the Government's spurious claim regarding 'weapons of mass destruction' (WMD).

This phrase was so frequently used by the Government – and repeated so often by our newspapers – that the American Dialect Society chose 'weapons of mass destruction' as the 2002 word (or phrase) of the year;

the more significant term, 'patriotism' – given its own ubiquity in the media – was surely running a close second, and was clearly a subject to be found in many of Woolf's writings. In addition to *Three Guineas*, these would include her novels, diary entries, letters and many essays, such as 'Thoughts on Peace in an Air Raid'. Woolf was quite sceptical about the newspapers of her day and expressed strong feelings about the Northcliffe Press in both her diaries and letters. These newspapers were controlled by the politically conservative Alfred Charles Harmsworth, a figure not unlike today's Rupert Murdoch, with his equally conservative media empire. Examining these two media strongholds, we can certainly see the linkage between Woolf's astute and sometimes scathing commentary on the newspapers of her day and our own sceptical assessments of today's print and visual media. These connections also highlight the current problems of corporate media ownership, including television stations and Internet companies, not present during Woolf's lifetime. As she experienced during World War I, people on both sides of the Atlantic have been absolutely bombarded with varied forms of the word 'patriotism', by both governments and newspapers. It has become the word most often used to rationalise the massive use of violence and, simultaneously, to stifle all kinds of dissent. Today, this propaganda effort, which began during World War I, continues.

In studying Woolf's writings, we unfortunately recognise that our governments' strategic use of the words 'nation',[1] 'patriotism', 'freedom' and 'democracy', amongst others, have, to use a Woolfian phrase, 'pargetted' the information we are entitled to in our so-called 'democracies', and fabricated new information – 'disinformation' – in order to fulfill their political agendas. To assess how this was both expressed and enacted during Woolf's lifetime I will refer to several significant works from that period. They include: Leo Tolstoy's 'Christianity and Patriotism' (1894) and 'Patriotism and Government' (1900), Walter Lippmann's *Public Opinion* (1922), Edward Bernays's *Propaganda* (1928) and Arthur Ponsonby's *Falsehood in Wartime: Propaganda Lies of the First World War* (1928). Of these, Lippmann's and Ponsonby's works were part of Leonard and Virginia Woolf's library. And although all were published between 1894 and 1928, their prescience regarding the problematic relationship between propaganda and democracy makes them indispensable. Arthur Ponsonby, in 1928, clearly predicted our present media problems:

> In future wars we have now to look forward to a new and far more efficient instrument of propaganda – the Government control of broadcasting. Whereas . . . in the past we have used the word 'broadcast' symbolically as meaning the efforts of the Press and individual reporters, in future we must

use the word literally, since falsehood can now be circulated universally, scientifically, and authoritatively. (27)

This discussion begins with an example from an American newspaper, since our current media problems seem to resonate so clearly with what Woolf began to call 'those damned newspapers' (*LII* 90). On 26 May 2004, *The New York Times* was forced to publish a quasi-apology due to the shoddy journalism of several of its reporters; the articles in question had to do with the newspaper's coverage of the lead-up to the war in Iraq. Although the apology/explanation did not go far enough – and was buried on page A10 – it did generate some good critical discussions in other magazines and journals, such as *The Nation* and *The New York Review of Books*; these articles served to precipitate an in-depth investigation into the complete failure of the press during the lead-up to the war in Iraq. One could easily conclude from the information revealed that *The New York Times*, the so-called 'newspaper of record' in the USA and around the world, was actually complicit with the US Government in supporting the decision to go to war. A terrible silence seemed to prevail at many major newspapers – almost a fear of speaking out. Was there a need, some other journals asked, post 9/11, to maintain a certain 'patriotism', or were these newspapers (including *The Washington Post*) simply going for the 'scoop', getting any story – without solid evidence – before a competitor did? Or were they censoring stories because of government intervention? What became and remains the more significant story – during Woolf's time and the present – is the reporting about the reporting, and the increasingly complex relationship between government and the media.

In one major example of the failure of *The New York Times*, a senior reporter, Judith Miller, not named but referred to in the apology, wrote articles before the war quoting government sources (Paul Wolfowitz, Richard Perle and Douglas Feith, as well as Ahmed Chalabi, head of the Iraqi National Congress) with whom she had long-standing personal and professional relationships; many of these articles were about WMD.[2] During television and print interviews, Vice President Dick Cheney often referred to the information contained in the *New York Times* articles written by Miller in order to buttress his case for the presence of these weapons. This set up a loop in which Cheney's minions placed information on to the front page of *The New York Times*, and he gained credibility by essentially quoting himself and his colleagues – and disseminating false information to the world. With this unfortunate situation in mind, I would like to show how the newspapers in Woolf's time – especially leading up to the two World Wars – were as unreliable and unscrupulous as those we now read on a daily basis.

Woolf clarified this point for us in *Three Guineas*:

> if you want to know any fact about politics you must read at least three different newspapers, compare at least three different versions of the same fact, and come in the end to your own conclusion. . . . In other words, you have to strip each statement of its money motive, of its power motive, of its advertisement motive, of its publicity motive, of its vanity motive, let alone all of the other motives, which, as an educated man's daughter, are familiar to you, before you make up your mind about which fact about politics to believe. (145–8)

That many major newspapers and media outlets are now publicly owned companies with corporate philosophies that look to increasing readership, advertising and the financial bottom line – as *Three Guineas* asserts – has transformed them, resulting in the frequent blurring of 'news' and 'entertainment'. Although 'journalistic' practices continue to evolve, along with cultural changes, they have always had their problematic aspects. This is clearly evident when one reads Leo Tolstoy's negative ideas regarding the newspapers of his day.

Woolf's commentary about the press in *Three Guineas* shares a great deal with the ideas Tolstoy presented in his 1900 essay, 'Patriotism and Government',[3] and his comments on 'war', 'outsider' status, 'pacifism' and 'patriotism' resonate with many of Woolf's political and philosophical ideas. Of course, Woolf both read and wrote about Tolstoy's writings, later helping to translate several of his works for the Hogarth Press; and since *The Kingdom of God and Peace Essays* was published by Oxford University Press in 1936, and the Woolfs owned many of Tolstoy's texts, one can assume a certain familiarity with his ideas.

As my epigraph from 'Patriotism and Government' suggests, Tolstoy, like Woolf, had serious concerns about the 'buying' of the press and how that related to the propagation of 'patriotism'. As he states: 'Patriotism and its results – wars – give an enormous revenue to the newspaper trade, and profits to many other trades.' This assured that

> the ruling classes have in their hands the army, money, the schools, the churches, and the press. In the schools, they kindle patriotism in the children by means of histories describing their own people as the best of all peoples and always in the right. Among adults they kindle it by spectacles, jubilees, monuments and by a lying patriotic press. (4)

Woolf's narrator echoes some of Tolstoy in *Three Guineas* when she vows that women are

> to take no share in patriotic demonstrations; to make no part of any claque or audience that encourages war; to absent herself from military displays, tournaments, tattoos, prize-givings and all such ceremonies as encourage

the desire to impose 'our' civilization or 'our' dominion upon other people. (166)

Like Woolf, Tolstoy railed against any imposed silence, and found that 'governments fear expression of independent thought more than an army' and so they 'seize control of churches and schools' and find ways to 'establish censorship' and 'bribe newspapers' (Tolstoy, 'Christianity and Patriotism', 532).

Woolf, a pacifist like Tolstoy, had her counterpart in Francis Meynell, a conscientious objector in WWI who anticipated Woolf's attack on militarist conditioning in *Three Guineas*:

> the martial music, the medals, the religious blessing of banners, the uniforms to catch the eye of the child , the picture of the soldier always as a saviour, not as a destroyer – it is by ruses and disguises such as these that the adult mind is rendered childish, and the horror and pain and frustration and crippling of war are made a schoolboy's holiday. (Meynell 137)

More recently, in his 2003 book, *War is a Force that Gives us Meaning*, Chris Hedges, a war correspondent for *The New York Times*, talks about 'patriotism' as 'often a thinly veiled form of collective self-worship, that celebrates our goodness, our ideals, our mercy and bemoans the per-fidiousness of those who hate us' (10). Hedges sees war as an attempt to make the world understandable, a black and white tableau of 'us' and 'them'. In her writings on *The Origins of Totalitarianism*, Hannah Arendt speaks of these simplistic divisions, 'for whoever is not included is excluded, whoever is not with me is against me, so the world loses all the nuance and pluralistic aspects that [they assume] have become too confusing for the masses' (380–1). Woolf, in her resistance to binary oppositions and to labels that tend to 'constrict', sets out in *Three Guineas* to undermine and resist the same clear-cut ways of thinking.

Utilisation of the word 'patriotic', in all of its guises, serves govern-ments well, for it reiterates the 'us' and 'them' mentality, the necessary division of the 'patriotic' from the 'unpatriotic'. Re-reading *Three Guineas* in 2009, in the throes of our own six-and-one-half-year war in Iraq, we also read and listen to our present 'prostituted fact-purveyors' and their constant invocation of 'patriotism'. We also note the use of this word, with its roots in *patria*, or fatherland, in the Government's naming of the 'Patriot Act' in October of 2001. It is quite ironic to use the word 'Patriot' to name an act that deprives people of many consti-tutional rights by giving the executive branch of the government new powers of search and surveillance, and indefinite detention of citizens and non-citizens without formal charges; it is an act that impinges on free speech, due process and equal protection under the law.[4]

Woolf's sense of 'patriotism' and its connection to war is evident in some early letters and diary entries. In a 1915 diary entry, after attending a concert at Queen's Hall, where it was customary to open the concert with the National Anthem and follow it with a hymn, 'O God our Strength', Woolf wrote: 'I think patriotism is a base emotion. By this I mean that they played a national Anthem & a Hymn, & all I could feel was the entire absence of emotion in myself & everyone else' (*DI* 5). Regarding the same concert, she wrote to Duncan Grant, 'What hellish luck – to miss you – and all for the sake of a Queen's Hall concert, where the patriotic sentiment was so revolting that I was nearly sick' (*LII* 57). As Karen Levenback points out in *Virginia Woolf and the Great War*, 'What we see in her wartime writings . . . is a movement toward understanding that the sense of immunity for the effects of war – shared by much of the civilian population – was an illusion.' The war for both civilians and would-be combatants, had been fictionalized through 'the tyranny of the Northcliffe Press' (10, 13) and mythologised in a history that was, in Woolf's words, 'all morality and battles' (*DII* 115). Levenback also suggests that Woolf felt the Government and the press were engaged in a conspiracy aimed at hoodwinking the unthinking young, such as Rupert Brooke, and Cecil and Philip Woolf, into becoming players in the drama of war (13).

The 'damned newspapers' (*LII* 90) that Woolf referred to, were – as noted above – owned and controlled by Lord Alfred Charles William Harmsworth, or the first Viscount Northcliffe. Like Rupert Murdoch, who owns 275 newspapers and many television and radio stations on three continents, including the *New York Post* and Fox News Corp, Northcliffe held the largest media empire at that time and utilised it to impart his conservative vision. Its effect on Woolf is expressed in her diary in 1918:

> The Northcliffe papers do all they can to insist upon the indispensability & delight of war. They magnify our victories to make our mouths water for more; they shout with joy when the Germans sink the Irish mail; but they do also show some signs of apprehension that Wilson's terms may be accepted. (*DI* 200)

Phillip Knightley comments on this function of newspapers in *The First Casualty*: 'The willingness of newspaper proprietors to accept this control [government censorship] and their co-operation in disseminating propaganda brought them the rewards of social rank and political power. But it also undermined the public faith in the press' (80–1).

Many questions regarding self-censorship at *The New York Times* provoked a heated response in the Letters to the Public Editor column.

On 16 December 2005, the paper revealed that the publication of a report on the Bush Administration's 'warrantless surveillance of communications' had been 'delayed for a year'. The executive editor, Bill Keller, had met with senior Administration officials about their concerns and made the decision not to publish at that time. It was later revealed that the 'delay' was actually fourteen months, and that this new time-frame created the potential for influencing the 2004 presidential election results. As one letter notes: 'Mr. Keller's job as executive editor of *The Times* is not to influence elections. It is not to decide what is "fair" to politicians (especially after including in his consideration of "fairness," consultation with the very administration accused of illegal activities)' (Calame 10). Many readers expressed disappointment with the newspaper and voiced concern that the editorial staff was perhaps 'embedded' with the Government.

In Frank Rich, however, an OP-ED columnist for *The New York Times*, we have a journalist who reveals what the public needs to know. Recently, he took his readers back a few years: 'In the run-up to the war . . . the administration did not even bother to commission an N.I.E., a summary of the latest findings from every American intelligence agency, on Iraq's weapons.' The answer, he reminds us, is found in

> the most revealing war document leaked to date: the Downing Street memo of 23 July 2002, written eight months before the invasion. In that secret report to the Blair government, the head of British intelligence reported on a trip to Washington, where he learned that the Bush administration was fixing the 'intelligence and facts' around the predetermined policy of going to war with Iraq. If we were going to fix the intelligence anyway, there was no need for an N.I.E. (10).

That this highly significant event received such minimal coverage in the American press after it was leaked in May 2005, and, more importantly, that the American public showed so little interest in it, indicates how effective the Bush Administration's 'culture of deception' and 'manufacture of consent' has been. As Rich asserts: 'This is the history we must remember now more than ever, because it keeps repeating itself, with ever more tragic results' (10).

Interestingly, Rupert Murdoch's father, Keith Murdoch, was involved in fighting the pervasive censorship of the British press during the battle of Gallipoli. He turned over suppressed information regarding this disaster to the British Government and tried to rectify the serious problem of war correspondents at the time – for they were the first victims of propaganda in WWI (Knightley 100–3). Although many informed individuals took a stand against WWI and demanded a moral reason for the war, the Government simply had none (Knightley

81). The Government had to create animosity against the Germans and their propaganda machine worked so well that twenty years later Joseph Goebbels based his propaganda on Britain's. Lord Northcliffe, proprietor of *The Times* and the *Daily Mail*, and 'the Director of Propaganda in Enemy Countries', was known to the Germans as 'the Minister of Lying', and from Woolf's statements one assumes she agreed with them. As Knightley suggests: 'The war was made to appear as one of defense versus a menacing aggressor' (82). The *Daily Mail*, Northcliffe's paper, referred to the Kaiser in just one article as a 'lunatic', 'barbarian', 'madman', 'monster' and 'criminal monarch' (82). Political leaders joined the propaganda campaign. Atrocities were fabricated. Northcliffe told his editors: 'The allies must never be tired of insisting that they are the victims of a deliberate aggression' (83). *The New York Times* took action to stop a rumour that it was partially controlled by the *Times of London* and that Lord Northcliffe was dictating *New York Times* policy to make it friendly to Britain and hostile to Germany (119). By 1919, Woolf wrote in her diary about the possibility of someone buying back the *Times of London*, 'to make it into a decent paper again' (*DI* 254). The 'lying patriotic press', in Tolstoy's words, continued to exploit the citizenry.

Given this activity, questions were raised about the accuracy of reporting and its connections to the functioning of democracy in Walter Lippmann's *Public Opinion*. As Ronald Steel asks in his Foreword to Lippmann's 1922 work: 'How could the public get the information it needed to make rational political judgments if it could not rely on the press?' (xi). *Public Opinion*, which seems to foreshadow some ideas in Woolf's 'Craftsmanship' and *Three Guineas*, is, although extremely controversial in many ways, quite relevant to today's questions about the shaping of public opinion. Lippmann was interested in the psychological forces involved in forming opinions, and how these opinions could be shaped (xii). 'Troubled by what he had learned as a wartime propagandist, [Lippmann] had come to believe that distortion of information was inescapable.' According to Steel, 'buried in Lippmann's measured, rational prose was a stunning rejection of traditional theories of democracy and the role played by the press' (xii, xiv).

Lippmann, before becoming a famous journalist, met Leonard Woolf while travelling to a Fabian Society meeting in 1914. In *Beginning Again*, Leonard Woolf describes their train ride to this meeting; here they spoke at length about Freud's writings, Leonard having just read *The Interpretation of Dreams* and reviewed *The Psychopathology of Everyday Life* (*Beginning* 167–8). Lippmann's familiarity with Freud's ideas is evident in his description of Freudians in *Public Opinion*:

They have assumed that if internal derangements could be straightened out, there would be little or no confusion about what is the obviously normal relationship. But public opinion deals with indirect, unseen, and puzzling facts, and there is nothing obvious about them. The situations to which public opinions refer are known only as opinions. (17)

Lippmann's scepticism, like Woolf's, relates to the problems inherent in language and the subsequent difficulties of communication. For Lippmann, 'words, like currency, are turned over and over again, to evoke one set of images to-day, another tomorrow. There is no certainty whatever that the same word will call out exactly the same idea in the reader's mind as it did in the reporter's' (Lippmann 42). In writing of Lloyd George, he says: 'A British Prime Minister, speaking in English to the whole attentive world, speaks his own meaning in his own words, to all kinds of people who will see *their* meaning in those words' (42–3; emphasis mine). Lippmann's comments about language are similar to those in Virginia Woolf's essay, 'Craftsmanship'. Here, 'words do not live in dictionaries; they live in the mind' (204) and 'they mean one thing to one person, another thing to another person; they are unintelligible to one generation, plain as pikestaff to the next' (206). Lippmann finds that

the ideas which we allow the words we read to evoke form the biggest part of the original data of our opinions. The world is vast, the situations that concern us are intricate, the messages are few, and the biggest part of opinion must be constructed in the imagination. (44)

Ultimately, Lippmann believes that the complexities of our world should not be left to the public to interpret, and that one should have so-called 'experts' as intermediaries who would help people make their political decisions. This aspect of his work is most problematic, for who are these 'experts' and who selects them? What does that say about democracy? For Lippmann, there were the 'insiders', specialists with the knowledge to act, and there were those without 'the time, nor attention, nor interest, nor the equipment for specific judgment'. These are the 'outsiders' (251). And, according to Lippmann, every one of us is an outsider to all but a few aspects of modern life. 'It is on the men inside, working under conditions that are sound, that the daily administrations of society must rest' (251). Perhaps Woolf's 'Outsider Society', with its ethic of resistance, stems from her response to Lippmann's very controlling insiders. Clearly her writings both express and enact resistance to these 'men on the inside', 'the inner circle', those doing the 'deciding' – like George Bush's labelling of himself as 'the Decider' ('Bush: "I'm the Decider"'). Lippmann's call for this kind of coercion, with its concomitant erasure, was clearly undemocratic and many were disturbed by his ideas.

Lippmann's philosophy at that time, which supposedly changed in later years, seems to be echoed by both the Bush and Blair Administrations. When huge numbers of 'outsiders' (in a Woolfian sense) voiced their opinions about the potential attack on Iraq in the many anti-war demonstrations around the world in 2003, the US President referred to them as 'focus groups' ('Bush Unswayed'), clearly reflecting the 'marketing' of this war to the public; the outsiders' 'focus groups', however, were totally ignored. What is certain is that the 'selling' of the Iraq War has been masterful; the propaganda effort, with its manipulation of language, blatant lies, constant linkage of Iraq to '9/11', and the necessary inculcation of 'fear', was brilliant. This is the 'mission' that the Bush Administration 'accomplished'.

And yet, one is always shocked at how intensely the populace is drawn in by the sales pitch. The watchdog role of the press in a democracy seems diminished, and the search for 'news' that is not, as Woolf states in *Three Guineas*, 'prostituted' or 'adulterated', is quite time-consuming. It is difficult to 'read between the lines', to translate the subtext from the distorted language used to 'propagate' this war. That the term 'propaganda' comes from the word 'propagate' is no surprise.

Edward Bernays, a nephew of Sigmund Freud, originally published his treatise, *Propaganda*, in New York in 1928. Influenced by Freud and by Lippmann's earlier work on public opinion, Bernays felt that 'the conscious and intelligent manipulation of the organized habits and opinions of the masses is an important element in democratic society. Those who manipulate this unseen mechanism of society constitute an invisible government which is the true ruling power of our country' (37). Bernays sounds very much like Lippmann here as he re-emphasises that 'we are governed, our minds molded, our tastes formed, our ideas suggested, largely by men we have never heard of.' These are the 'invisible governors', and 'it is they who pull the wires which control the public mind' (37–8). Many also see the Bush Administration in this light, for its arrogance, its secrecy and its absolute refusal to answer questions on issues that are clearly in the public domain; its ability to manipulate both the media and the population is impressive, even to those in the Democratic Party.

Bernays, according to Mark Crispin Miller's Introduction, 'casts himself as a supreme manipulator, *mastering* the responses of a pliable, receptive population'. And although the image of the detached propagandist was not Bernays's idea, 'that cool and manly image was a commonplace from the Twenties through the Cold War, as was the obverse image of "the crowd" as *female* in its feverish responsiveness' (20, 21). According to Miller, 'this tableau of domination' clearly resonates with 'the unmoved mover' and 'that spellbinder who excites the vulgar herd' (21). It certainly has links with the Dictator from *Three Guineas* who will 'dictate to other human beings how they shall live; what they shall do' (80), as well as the demonising and exclusion of women portrayed in that work. One also finds connections with the so-called smooth and 'civilised' controlling of the 'wild' and 'barbaric', as found in *A Room of One's Own* and so many of Woolf's writings. Woolf seems to have an understanding of Bernays's methods – methods from Freud's writings.

Miller asserts in his Introduction to *Propaganda*:

> Although the practice had, albeit unnamed, been variously used by governments for centuries . . . it was not until 1915 that governments systematically deployed the entire range of modern media to rouse their populations to fanatical assent. Here was an extraordinary state accomplishment: mass enthusiasm at the prospect of a global brawl that otherwise would mystify those very masses, and that shattered most of those who actually took part in it. The Anglo-American drive to demonise 'the Hun', and to cast the war as a transcendent clash between Atlantic 'civilization' and Prussian 'barbarism,' made so powerful an impression on so many that the worlds of government and business were forever changed. (11, 12)

A book in the Woolfs' library, Arthur Ponsonby's 1928 *Falsehood in Wartime: Propaganda Lies of the First World War* begins with the recognition that 'falsehood is a recognized and extremely useful weapon in warfare, and every country uses it quite deliberately to deceive its own people, to attract neutrals, and to mislead the enemy.' But what Ponsonby, a Member of Parliament and a pacifist, finds most troubling is 'the amazing readiness to believe. It is, indeed, because of human credulity that lies flourish' (13). Interestingly, he finds the need for the weapon of falsehood 'more necessary in a country where military conscription is not the law of the land than in countries where the manhood of the nation is automatically drafted into the Army, Navy, or Air Service. The public can be worked up emotionally by sham ideals' (14). Here Ponsonby describes all the necessary actions: 'Facts must be distorted, relevant circumstances concealed, and a picture presented which by its crude colouring will persuade the ignorant people that their Government is blameless, their cause is righteous, and that the indisputable wickedness of the enemy has been proved beyond question' (15). Of course, this could be a description of what is happening today in the USA or Britain. Ponsonby, unlike Bernays, catalogues many of the major falsehoods propagated by the Allied Governments.[5] As a pacifist, he tried to reveal that 'war is fought in this fog of falsehood, a great deal of it undiscovered and accepted as truth. . . . Any attempt to doubt or deny even the most fantastic story has to be condemned at once as unpatriotic, if not traitorous' (16).

Perhaps avoidance of this 'fog of falsehood' is similar to the firm espousal of both Woolf and Tolstoy that one must refuse to allow oneself to be 'hypnotised'. In Tolstoy's 'Patriotism and Government', he calls for 'shaking off the hypnotism of patriotism' (13). Woolf shares Tolstoy's resistance to 'the power of medals, symbols, orders and even, it would seem, of decorated ink-pots to hypnotize the human mind [for] it must be our aim not to submit ourselves to such hypnotism' (*TG* 114). The American flag, along with the flag lapel pins worn by so many men, falls into this category.

In *Three Guineas*, Woolf, in response to this propagandising effort, envisions a woman-run newspaper that would be 'committed to a conspiracy, not of silence, but of speech' (91). She implements this idea in 'Thoughts on Peace in an Air Raid', as her narrator speaks of 'a woman in *The Times* this morning – a woman's voice saying, "Women have not a word to say in politics"' (*DM* 244). Later in that essay, this woman is identified as Lady Astor, who refers to '"women of ability" and how they "are held down because of a subconscious Hitlerism in the hearts of men"' (*DM* 245). Women and others excluded from what is considered to be a nation have no cause to be patriotic, 'no wish to be English as you yourself are English' (*TG* 154). Woolf's narrator calls for a different kind of connection to one's country, for this is definitely not her 'civilisation' (*DIV* 298). And as Woolf reiterates in a diary entry in 1940: 'I don't like any of the feelings war breeds: patriotism . . . all sentimental & emotional parodies of our real feelings' (*DV* 302).

While Woolf denigrated both 'patriotism' and 'nationalism', she seems to have aligned herself with a certain 'cosmopolitanism'; she would also agree, however, that all of these terms are constantly in flux and undergoing revision. We are reminded of her narrator in 'Craftsmanship' explaining that words cannot be 'pinned down to one meaning' (*DM* 206). And we learn from Homi Bhabha, in *Nation and Narration*, and from recent works that refuse to define 'cosmopolitanism',[6] that terms such as these have multiple meanings, each expressing and enacting complicated histories and varied trajectories. This is evident as we consider Woolf's oft-quoted statement from *Three Guineas*: 'as a woman I have no country; as a woman I want no country; as a woman, my country is the whole world' (166).

This statement has been used in varying forms, and in differing contexts, by Diogenes, Socrates, Thomas Paine, Oliver Goldsmith, Henry David Thoreau and William Lloyd Garrison, amongst others; Garrison, an American Abolitionist, used a variation of this quotation as the motto of his 'Non-Resistance Society'. His son, also William Lloyd, found similarities between Tolstoy's anti-war works and his father's ideas of 1838, and sent Tolstoy the 'Declaration of Sentiments' from William Lloyd Garrison's meeting to create the 'New England Non-Resistance Society'. This document contained their motto: 'Our country is the world, our countrymen are all mankind' (*The Liberator* 154). Given Tolstoy's stance against war and weaponry, and his philosophy of 'non-resistance', which attracted Gandhi, he included Garrison's motto is his 1894 work, *The Kingdom of God is Within You*. Both Tolstoy's 'non-resistance' and Woolf's philosophy of 'indifference' share a call for 'resistance', a call 'not to fight with arms', a call to resist 'slavery' in all it guises (*TG* 162–5). For Tolstoy, the action is 'to turn the other cheek', and for Woolf, the move is be 'outside', in a place of complete 'indifference'. Both would 'take no share in patriotic demonstrations' (162–5) and agree that 'to be passive is to be active' (170). This stance involves 'the power of outsiders to abolish or modify other institutions of which they disapprove, whether public dinners, public speeches, Lord Mayors' banquets and other obsolete ceremonies [which] are pervious to indifference and will yield to its pressure' (181).

Woolf's narrator, when speaking of being 'outside', of having 'no country', was identifying herself as 'cosmopolitan'; and as Alex Zwerdling suggests, 'Woolf's cultural loyalties were European rather than British' (277). This, however, is a narrowly defined 'cosmopolitanism', as indicated by the provocative responses to Martha Nussbaum's 'Patriotism and Cosmopolitanism'. Collected in *For Love of Country?*, along with sixteen responses representing extremely varied philosophical views, this work exemplifies the problematic nature of language that Woolf so often explores.

Nussbaum examines the Stoics and their ideas for 'a citizen of the world'; for them, 'one does not need to give up local identifications, but to think of oneself as surrounded by a series of concentric circles . . . and work to make all human beings part of our community of dialogue and concern' (9). Many of the respondents describe their own specific 'patriotism', defining it for themselves as Woolf's narrator does in *Three Guineas* (164). Perhaps this expresses what Woolf is doing as she writes to Ethel Smyth following the publication of *Three Guineas*, in order to discuss young men and war, and to define her 'patriotism':

> Patriotism. My dear E . . . of course I'm 'patriotic': that is English, the language, farms, dogs, people: only we must enlarge the imaginative, and take stock of the emotion. And I'm sure I can; because I'm an outsider partly; and can get outside the vested interest better than Leonard even – tho' a Jew. (*LVI* 235)

Resisting 'patriotism', Woolf's narrator in her 1940 essay, 'Thoughts on Peace in An Air Raid', calls for 'thinking against the current' (243), against the loudspeakers, the Government, and the newspapers that may be the voices of that Government. This 'official story' must be resisted, and Woolf, in so many of her writings, both expresses and enacts this resistance.

Always interested in multiple voices, in hybridity, in the kind of language, as mentioned in 'Craftsmanship', where 'Royal words mate with commoners; English words marry French words, German words, Indian words, Negro words' (205), Woolf clearly resists simplistic dichotomies of good and evil, and likes the meaning of the French-derived word, 'nuance' – as President Bush does not. Woolf wants to interrupt the 'unanimity' of the 'current' with questions, with dissent. She calls for speech instead of silence, with plans for 'finding new words' and 'creating new methods' (*TG* 219). But she is intent on maintaining her 'outsider' status, which enables differing perspectives. And as the world views the almost daily 'photographs of dead bodies and ruined houses' from so many different countries, and we see the photos of the torture victims of Abu Ghraib – as concealed by government and media – there is the shared acknowledgement that 'the picture is the picture of evil' and there is strong determination 'to do what we can to destroy that evil' (219). 'Patriotism', responsible for so much violence, labels, silences, isolates and ultimately deprives people of freedom. As Woolf's narrator so poignantly points out in 'Thoughts on Peace in an Air Raid': 'It is not true we are free' (*DM* 245). And too many of us, as we acknowledge the diminishing health of our 'so-called democracies', may soon be echoing that line.

Notes

1. Ernest Renan's 'What is a Nation?' was in Virginia Woolf's library.
2. See John MacArthur (2009), 'The Lies We Bought', *Columbia Journalism Review* (May/Jun.); Franklin Foer (2004), 'The Source of the Trouble', *New York Magazine* (7 Jun.); and Michael Massing (2004), 'Now They Tell Us', *The New York Review of Books* 51(3) (3 Feb.)
3. Tolstoy's (1900) 'Patriotism and Government' is collected in (1911), *Essays and Letters*, trans. Aylmer Maude, Oxford: Oxford University Press. The page references refer to the online version listed in the Bibliography.
4. The 'Patriot Act' was signed into law by George Bush on 26 October 2001. It called for indefinite detentions of immigrants suspected of domestic terrorism, and the searching without warrants of homes, telephones, e-mail, computers, libraries, and medical and financial records. It was renewed in 2005 by the Bush Administration, with few changes and little opposition in Congress.
5. Arthur Ponsonby, Member of Parliament, wrote *Falsehood in Wartime: Propaganda Lies of the First World War* in 1928. It was published in London

by George Allen & Unwin. In 1980 and 1991, the Institute for Historical Review, thought to be a 'Holocaust denial' organisation, re-published this work.

6. See Carol A. Breckinridge, Sheldon Pollock, Homi Bhabha and Dipesh Chakrabarty (eds) (2002), 'Cosmopolitantinomies', *Cosmopolitanism*, Durham, NC: Duke University Press.

'Thinking Against the Current'

> Our resistance has to begin with a refusal to accept the legitimacy of the US occupation of Iraq. It means acting to make it materially impossible for empire to achieve its aims. It means soldiers should refuse to fight, reservists should refuse to serve, workers should refuse to load ships and aircraft with weapons.
>
> Arundhati Roy, *An Ordinary Person's Guide to Empire*[1]

Resistance, with its inextricable connection to freedom, expressed and enacted by the 'essayistic', plays a crucial role in this study and, most importantly, in our lives today. But questions abound. Has it become more difficult today to resist the 'official story' – the reporting of corporate/government fraud (almost inseparable), military cover-ups, torture, extraordinary rendition, indefinite detention, loss of constitutional rights, increasing violence against women, war crimes, slavery and more – or have we been too overwhelmed to focus? In some ways, the shocking conditions seem to be awakening certain segments of the populace but the level of complacency is still frightening. It is troubling to find that there is no outrage, except for the consistent cry: 'Where is the outrage?'

Woolf's call for participation, for activity, for critical thinking and critical reading seems quite urgent today, and we do see glimmers of hope as we watch sit-ins, reminiscent of the 1960s, and individuals with enormous courage who risk their lives to fight oppression. When Woolf asks in a 1937 diary entry: 'Why does one like the frantic and the unmastered?' (*DV* 116), she alludes to her admiration for the sheer power of nature – to the energy, freedom and resistance that inhere in this mode of being; her significant calls for acts of refusal are aligned with 'the frantic and the unmastered' – with wildness and freedom.

Today, more than ever, we have a US Government in place with increased executive power (achieved during the eight years of the Bush Administration). Presidents that follow rarely give up such newly found powers, but an independent press should be able to confront and to counter these potentially oppressive forces. Our press, in economic difficulty and having the added problems of media consolidation and competition from other media, does not play its clearly defined role in our democracy, but too frequently takes the position of echoing our government's agenda. In April 2008, *The New York Times* published a lengthy front-page article about the hiring of retired generals[2] to act as experts on television news programmes – as seemingly independent analysts of Iraq and Afghanistan – while being paid by the Pentagon and defence contractors to sell the Government's 'talking points' to the public. Fortunately, there are individuals doing good investigative journalism, but one needs to find them – to seek them out. These reporters must be, in Woolf's words, 'outside and critical', and not 'embedded' with the troops or socialising with the senators and congresspersons they plan to investigate the next day. Woolf's writings convey – in a multitude of contexts – that the smooth and conventional must be refused, while the rough and the 'wild' will go a long way towards helping us 'see', in the fullest sense of that word. Her narrator's invocation to 'observe', occurring six times in her essay, 'Montaigne', speaks both to looking within, to the 'inner life', what is referred to as 'the soul' in this work, and to examining our world, its leaders, and those in a position to provide you with the information so crucial in a democracy.

The beginning of this century has seen a continuing increase in the use of the new media, as new blogs appear by the thousands every week. The problem of discerning the reliability of the information made available is addressed by Woolf's narrator in *Three* Guineas. Here, we find her rationale for reading at least three dailies and three weeklies:

> each paper is financed by a board; that each board has a policy; that each board employs writers to expound that policy, and if writers do not agree with that policy, the writers, as you may remember . . . find themselves unemployed in the street. (*TG* 95)

Today, we have the ability to assess coverage of the same story from many papers within our own country, as well as to examine coverage from abroad. It is interesting to find that *The New York Times*, the so-called 'newspaper of record' for the world, has refused to cover certain politically difficult stories or has buried them in the back of the paper. Reading news of the same event from different countries around the world is surely enlightening – especially if one goes to *Al Jazeera* in English, *Haaretz* in Israel, *The Jerusalem Post* in Israel, and *The New York Times*, *The Guardian* and many others available online. In combination with those, one goes to one's chosen 'blogs' and newsletters – such as *Salon*, *Tom-Dispatch* and *Counterpunch* – to name a few from my 'home page'. It takes time to find out what is happening. What has been concealed may turn up sixty-four years later, as Daniel Ellsberg's[3] revelations on the bombings of Hiroshima and Nagasaki will attest. But what if one does not have access to the Internet, cannot afford a computer, cannot get to a library? As a *Guardian* editorial conveyed:

> Numerous towns and cities are waking up to the prospect that, for the first time since the Enlightenment, they may have to live without a verifiable source of information. David Simon, the creator of the Baltimore TV series, *The Wire*, warned at the weekend of the parallel story in the United States: 'Its got to be one of the dreams of American corruption.' (31 March 2009)

But for the others, 'information' is flowing from millions of blogs, citizen journalists, Twitter feeds, and other social media formats. As most of the world watched an almost two-year presidential campaign with minute-by-minute coverage, those who would be voting made decisions based on marketing, packaging, focus groups, and our interpretation of a totally orchestrated narrative that was movingly presented to us. Thinking about that campaign process, perhaps the words with which I began this study – Montaigne's motto – express what we feel so deeply today: 'Que sais-je?'

For Woolf, that kind of 'hypnotism' (*TG* 114) must be avoided; we must be awake to the language, to how it functions and to placing ourselves outside, having some distance – in a Brechtian sense – so that we may truly 'see', in a new way. Woolf's resistance to war, and her narrator's frightening descriptions of the drone-like sound of planes and bombs in 'Thoughts on Peace in an Air Raid', strike a chord today. But witnessing and experiencing bombings – as Virginia Woolf notes in her diary – is quite horrific: 'I've got it fairly vivid – the sensation: but cant [sic] see anything but suffocating nonentity following after' (*DV* 326). With our advanced technology, our 'military' in Langley, Virginia, using video game controls (a joystick), can send Predator drones armed with two 'Hellfire' missiles – each weigh 500 pounds – to Pakistan, although we have no declared war there. The 'suffocating nonentity' is certainly the result, but it is sold to the public as being quite clinical – the 'surgical strikes' of years past.

In the past few months, these operations have been carried out by the US CIA and Blackwater, a private contractor hired by the Pentagon; what we have, according to the title of Jeremy Scahill's recent article in *The Nation*, is 'The Secret US War in Pakistan'.[4] The numbers of civilians killed in these attacks is increasing, as it becomes more palatable to send 'unmanned' aircraft to do the bombing. But the terminology of war still echoes, as these 'silent' weapons, which the US Air Force describes as 'MALE' (medium alternate long endurance), are used increasingly to be sophisticated 'killing machines' or 'a flying assassin'.

In President Barack Obama's acceptance of the Nobel Peace Prize (10 December 2009) in Oslo, Norway – just a week after he ordered 30,000 more troops to Afghanistan – he used the term 'just war', as he continued to justify the actions he has taken in Afghanistan, with no mention of Pakistan. It was a speech that is clearly opposed to Virginia Woolf's 'Thoughts on Peace in an Air Raid', an essay that wants to 'think peace into existence' and posits in its title thinking about peace in the context of war. Obama spoke of war in the context of peace, in the ironic context of accepting the Nobel Peace Prize – which is quite an undertaking. In the process, he invoked phrases that were reminiscent of George Bush. His finding that 'the instruments of war do have a role to play in preserving the peace' (Oslo, 10 December 2009)[5] became one of the 'sound bites', along with his quotations from Martin Luther King, Nelson Mandela and Gandhi.

I thought of Jane Addams, winner of the Nobel Peace Prize in 1931, and her 1915 commentary at the founding conference of the Women's Peace Party in Washington, DC, where she enumerated the many hidden costs of war that simple calculations do not measure (61–4).[6] According to Danielle Poe,[7] 'Addams' overall concern was that war destroys "sensitiveness to human life." War destroys this sensitiveness by diminishing the protection, the nurture, the fulfillment, the conservation, and the ascent of human life' (Poe 35). From Addams, we find many of the arguments against war that we still hear today – in economic terms – as she continues that argument in substantially more meaningful terms. Poe notes that the 'costs' for Addams

> serve as an important reminder that war takes its toll on some of the most fundamental relations of cooperation among people. Just war calculates the evil effects of war but does not define the evil effects of war broadly enough to account for the ways in which not only is justice compromised but sensitiveness to human life is compromised as well. (Poe 36).

It is important to note that Addams read Virginia Woolf's writings, beginning in the 1920s.[8]

In his Nobel Peace Prize speech, in the context of 'just war', Obama spoke of his responsibility for deploying thousands of young Americans, noting that 'some will kill, and some will be killed.' He then mentioned his awareness of the 'costs of war', but it seemed, in Obama's usage, that although he spoke of 'difficult questions about the relationship between war and peace, and our efforts to replace one with the other', he was not willing – given the political expediency hovering over his decision – to make that choice. His later justification of force, on humanitarian grounds, led to his statement that 'inaction tears at our conscience and can lead to more costly intervention later.' Clearly, the 'other' costs of war, as Jane Addams views the problem, are not going to be acknowledged by someone willing to compromise on this issue. There is an interesting statement in Woolf's essay, 'Montaigne', as she reflects on the latter's ideas regarding those in public service: 'We must respect those who sacrifice themselves in the public service, load them with honours, and pity them for allowing, as they must, the inevitable compromise; but for ourselves let us fly fame, honour, and all offices that put us under an obligation to others' (CRI 63). One cannot avoid thinking about President Obama, and many of our world leaders, as they make their many questionable decisions.

Danielle Poe finds that 'of the many flaws with "just war" theorising, perhaps the most damning is that just war doctrine tends to justify wars, albeit only truly defensive ones, at a time when we ought to be thinking about ways to eliminate wars' (33). There is no shortage of voices or theories on this subject, and they certainly show the complexities that have been extolled by all sides. Interestingly, these opposing voices, this mass of differing and nuanced opinion serves us well, as we think back to Woolf's words, to her calls for multiple perspectives, diverse voices, a sense of awareness, involvement, critical thinking and critical reading; this approach, modelled by her narrative and rhetorical strategies, will keep us moving, away from the complacency that afflicts so many, and will free some new voices to enter the fray.

As the first decade of the twenty-first century ends, the words of Virginia Woolf's *Three Guineas* still reverberate. While the repetitious rationales for 'just wars' and 'preemptive wars' fill our media screens, we continue the search for 'new words' and 'new methods' (*TG* 143) that will put an end to the 'photographs of dead bodies and ruined houses' (141) that permeate our lives. As we listen to the questions and answers of the Chilcot Inquiry into the British decision to enter the Iraq War, and to the questions and answers of the recent US Supreme Court (*Citizens United v. Federal Election Commission*) as they overturned precedent to give corporations the ultimate authority over elections and governing, we recognise the dire need for new questions, and that they be, most importantly, our questions -followed by our actions. In essayistic fashion, we must move in new directions, always positioning ourselves, in Woolf's words, 'against the current', and never taking our focus away from the power of words.

Notes

1. Arundhati Roy (2004), 'Do Turkeys enjoy Thanksgiving?', in *An Ordinary Person's Guide to Empire*, Boston, MA: South End Press, 94, quoted in *Hypatia* (2008), 23(2) (Apr.-Jun.), 43.
2. In 20 April 2008, *The New York Times* published a front-page story about the media's role as a conduit for Pentagon propaganda. More than seventy-five retired generals were hired as 'message force multipliers' to convey the Pentagon's 'talking points' in support of the Iraq War.
3. Daniel Ellsberg plans to reveal hidden material from the bombings of Hiroshima and Nagasaki in instalments at http://www.ellsberg.net and on Truthdig.
4. Jeremy Scahill continues his exposé of the covert operations in Pakistan and about the Blackwater private contractors in (2009), 'The Secret US War in Pakistan', *The Nation* (21/28 Dec.), 11–18.
5. The White House, Office of the Press Secretary, Acceptance speech for Nobel Peace Prize.
6. Reference to Addams's speech, 'What war is destroying', on the 'hidden costs of war', given at the founding conference of the Women's Peace Party in Washington, DC. In Addams (2003), *Essays and Speeches on Peace*, ed. Marilyn Fischer and Judy D. Whipps (Bristol: Thoemmes). Quoted in (2008), 'Replacing Just War Theory with an Ethics of Sexual Difference', *Hypatia* 23(2) (Apr.-Jun.), 35.
7. See Danielle Poe (2008), 'Replacing Just War Theory with an Ethics of Sexual Difference', *Hypatia* 23(2) (Apr.-Jun.).
8. See Katherine Joslin (2004), *Jane Addams: A Writer's Life*, Chicago, IL: University of Illinois Press.

Bibliography

Addams, Jane [1915] (2003), 'What War Is Destroying', in *Essays and Speeches on Peace*, ed. Marilyn Fischer and Judy D. Whipps, Bristol: Thoemmes

Adorno, T. W. (1984), 'The Essay as Form', trans. Bob Hullot-Kentor and Fredric Will, *New German Critique* 32, 151–71

Allan, Tuzyline (1999), 'Civilization, Its Pretexts, and Virginia Woolf's Imagination', in *Virginia Woolf and Communities*, *Selected Papers from the Eighth Annual Conference on Virginia Woolf*, ed. Jeanette McVicker and Laura Davis, New York, NY: Pace University Press, 117–27

Allen, Judith (1999), 'The Rhetoric of Performance in *A Room of One's Own*', in *Virginia Woolf and Communities*, *Selected Papers from the Eighth Annual Conference on Virginia Woolf*, ed. Jeanette McVicker and Laura Davis, New York, NY: Pace University Press, 289–96

—— (1993), 'Those Soul Mates: Virginia Woolf and Michel de Montaigne', in *Virginia Woolf: Themes and Variations*, *Selected Papers from the Second Annual Conference on Virginia Woolf*, ed. Vara Neverow-Turk and Mark Hussey, New York, NY: Pace University Press

Arendt, Hannah (1979), *The Origins of Totalitarianism*, San Diego, CA: Harcourt Brace

Bakhtin, M. M. (1981), *The Dialogic Imagination: Four Essays by M. M. Bakhtin*, ed. Michael Holquist, trans. Caryl Emerson and Michael Holquist, Austin, TX: University of Texas Press

—— (1973), *Problems of Dostoevsky's Poetics*, trans. R. W. Rotsel, Ann Arbor, MI: University of Michigan Press

Bauschatz, Cathleen M. (1994), 'A Reader-oriented Approach to Teaching Montaigne', *Approaches to Teaching Montaigne's Essays*, ed. Patrick Henry, New York, NY: LA

Beauvoir, Simone de (1952), *The Second Sex*, trans. H. M. Parshley, New York, NY: Knopf

Beer, Gillian (1996), *The Common Ground*, Ann Arbor, MI: University of Michigan Press

Benjamin, Walter (1969), *Illuminations*, ed. and intro. Hannah Arendt, trans. Harry Zohn, New York, NY: Schocken

Benstock, Shari (1991), *Textualizing the Feminine: On the Limits of Genre*, Norman, OK: University of Oklahoma Press

Bernays, Edward [1928] (2005), *Propaganda*, New York, NY: Ig

Bishop, Edward L. (1987), 'Metaphor and the Subversive Process of Virginia Woolf's Essays', *Style* 21(4) (Winter), 573–88

—— (1992), 'The Subject in *Jacob's Room*', *Modern Fiction Studies* 38(1), 147–75

Black, Naomi (2004), *Virginia Woolf as Feminist*, Ithaca, NY: Cornell University Press

Bornstein, George, ed. (1991), *Representing Modern Texts: Editing as Interpretation*, Ann Arbor, MI: University of Michigan Press

Bowlby, Rachel (1988), *Virginia Woolf: Feminist Destinations*, Oxford: Basil Blackwell

Bradshaw, David (2002), '"Vanished Like Leaves": The Military, Elegy and Italy in *Mrs Dalloway*', *WSA* 8, 107–25

Brodkey, Harold (1985), 'Reading is the Most Dangerous Game', *New York Times Book Review* (24 Nov.), 44

Brody, Jules (1994), 'Of the Art of Discussion: A Philological Reading', *Approaches to Teaching Montaigne's Essays*, ed. Patrick Henry, New York, NY: MLA, 159–65

Bromwich, David (2008), 'Euphemism and American Violence', *New York Review of Books* (3 Apr.), 28–30

Bulletin of the New York Public Library (1977), 80 (Winter)

'Bush: "I'm the Decider" on Rumsfeld' (2006). www.cnn.com/2006/POLITICS/04/18/rumsfeld/

'Bush Unswayed by Anti-War Demonstrations' (2003), *All Things Considered*, National Public Radio, WHYY, Philadelphia (18 Feb.)

Butler, Judith (2004), *Precarious Life: The Powers of Mourning and Violence*, New York, NY: Verso

Butrym, Alexander J. (1989), *Essays on the Essay: Redefining the Genre*, Athens, GA: University of Georgia Press

Calame, Byron (2006), Letters to the Public Editor, *The New York Times* (20 Aug.)

Carlston, Erin G. (1998), *Thinking Fascism: Sapphic Modernism and Fascist Modernity*, Stanford, CA: Stanford University Press

Caughie, Pamela (1991), *Virginia Woolf and Postmodernism*, Urbana, IL: University of Illinois Press

Cave, Terence (1987), 'Problems of Reading in the *Essais*', *Michel de Montaigne*, ed. Harold Bloom, New York, NY: Chelsea, 133–66

Celestin, Roger (1996), *From Cannibals to Radicals: Figures and Limits of Exoticism*, Minneapolis, MN: University of Minnesota Press

Culler, Jonathan (1975), *Structural Poetics*, Ithaca, NY: Cornell University Press

Danner, Mark (2009), 'US Torture: Voices from the Black Sites', *ICRC Report of Fourteen 'High Value Detainees' in CIA Custody*, International Committee of the Red Cross (Feb. 2007), *New York Review of Books* (9 April), 69–77

Deleuze, Gilles and Félix Guattari (1987), *A Thousand Plateaus: Capitalism and Schizophrenia*, trans. and foreword Brian Massumi, Minneapolis, MN: University of Minnesota Press

Desan, Philippe (1994), 'For a Sociology of the Essays', *Approaches to Teaching Montaigne's Essays*, ed. Patrick Henry, New York, NY: MLA, 90–7

Dusinberre, Juliette (1991), 'Virginia Woolf and Montaigne', *Textual Practice* 5(7), 219–41

Ellsberg, Daniel (2009), 'Hiroshima Day', *The Nation* (6 Aug.)

Emerson, Ralph Waldo (1850), 'Montaigne; or, the Skeptic', in *Representative Men*, London: Routledge

Felski, Rita (1988), *Beyond Feminist Aesthetics*, Boston, MA: Harvard University Press

Ferris, Paul (1972), *The House of Northcliffe*, New York, NY: World

Finer, Herman (1935), *Mussolini's Italy*, London: Gollancz

Fisher, Jane (1990), 'The Seduction of the Father: Virginia Woolf and Leslie Stephen', *Women's Studies* 18, 31–48

Fisher, John (1984), 'Entitling', *Critical Inquiry* (Dec.), 286–98

Flint, Kate (1996), 'Reading Uncommonly: Virginia Woolf and the Practice of Reading', *The Yearbook of English Studies* 26, 187–98

Fowler, Regina (2002), 'Virginia Woolf: Lexicographer', *English Language Notes* 39, 54–70

Friedrich, Hugo (1991), *Montaigne*, intro. Philippe Desan, trans. Dawn Eng, Berkeley, CA: University of California Press

Gallop, Jane (1982), *The Daughter's Seduction: Feminism and Psychoanalysis*, Ithaca, NY: Cornell University Press

Garrison, Willam Lloyd (1838), *The Liberator* (28 Sep.), 154

Gattens, Marie-Luise (1995), *Women Writers and Fascism*: *Reconstructing History*, Gainsville, FL: University Press of Florida

Gilbert, Sandra M. and Susan Gubar (1979), *Madwoman in the Attic*, New Haven, CT: Yale University Press

Goldman, Jane (2004), *Modernism, 1910–1945*, Hampshire: Palgrave Macmillan

Good, Graham (1988), *The Observing Self: Rediscovering the Essay*, London: Routledge

Habermas, Jurgen [1962] (1991), *The Structural Transformation of the Public Sphere: An Inquiry into a Category of Bourgeois Society*, Cambridge: Cambridge University Press

Haller, Evelyn (1992), 'Virginia Woolf and Katherine Mansfield: Or, the Case of the Déclassé Wild Child', *Virginia Woolf Miscellanies*, ed. Mark Hussey and Vara Neverow-Turk, 96–104

Hardison, O. B., Jr (1989), 'Binding Proteus: An Essay on the Essay', in *Essays on the Essay: Redefining the Genre*, ed. Alexander J. Butrym, Athens, GA: University of Georgia Press, 11–28

Harrison, Jane [1903] (1991), *Prolegomena to the Study of Greek Religion*, Princeton, NJ: Princeton University Press

Hedges, Chris (2002), *War is a Force that Gives us Meaning*, New York, NY: Public Affairs

Holdheim, William Wolfgang (1984), *The Hermeneutic Mode*, Ithaca, NY: Cornell University Press

Hughes, Geoffrey (2008), 'Words, War and Terror', *English Today* 24(1) (Mar.)

Hussey, Mark, ed. (1991), *Virginia Woolf and War: Fiction, Reality, And Myth*, New York, NY: Syracuse University Press

—— (1995), *Virginia Woolf A-Z*, New York, NY: Oxford University Press

Iser, Wolfgang (1978), *The Act of Reading*, Baltimore, MD: Johns Hopkins University Press

Johnson, Chalmers (2000), *Blowback*, New York, NY: Henry Holt

Johnston, Georgia (1997), 'Class Performance in *Between the Acts*: Audiences for Miss La Trobe and Mrs. Manresa', *Woolf Studies Annual* 3, 61–75

Kauffmann, R. Lane (1989), 'The Skewed Path: Essaying as Unmethodical Method', *Essays on the Essay*, ed. Alexander J. Butryn, Athens, GA: University of Georgia Press, 221–49

Kent, Thomas (1986), *Interpretation and Genre*, Lewisburg, PA: Bucknell University Press

Klaus, Carl H. (1990), 'On Virginia Woolf and the Essay', *Iowa Review* 20(2) (Spring/Summer), 28–34

Knightley, Phillip (1975), *The First Casualty*, New York, NY: Harcourt Brace Jovanovich

Kritzman, Lawrence D. (1983), 'My Body, My Text: Montaigne and the Rhetoric of Sexuality', *Journal of Medieval and Renaissance Studies* 13:1 (Spring), 81–95

Léry, Jean de (1975), *Histoire d'un voyage fait en la terre du Brésil*, Geneva: Droz

Levenback, Karen (1999), *Virginia Woolf and the Great War*, New York, NY: Syracuse University Press

Lewis, David (1994), 'Montaigne and Politics', *Approaches to Teaching Montaigne's Essays*, ed. Patrick Henry, New York, NY: MLA, 69–77

Lippmann, Walter [1922] (1997), *Public Opinion*, New York, NY: Simon & Schuster

Luckhurst, Nicola (1999), 'To Quote my Quotation from Montaigne', *Virginia Woolf Reading the Renaissance*, ed. Sally Green, Athens, OH: Ohio University Press

Lukács, Georg (1974), *Soul and Form*, trans. Anne Bostock, Cambridge, MA: Massachusetts Institute of Technology

MacArthur, John R. (2009), 'The Lies We Bought', *Columbia Journalism Review* (May/Jun.)

Marchi, Dudley M. (1993), 'Montaigne and the New World: The Cannibalism of Cultural Production', *Modern Language Studies* 23(4) (Autumn), 35–54

—————— (1997), 'Virginia Woolf Crossing the Borders of History, Culture, and Gender: The Case of Montaigne, Pater, and Gournay', *Comparative Literature Studies* 34:1, 1–30

Marshik, Celia (1999), 'Publication and "Public Women": Prostitution and Censorship in Three Novels by Virginia Woolf', *MFS* 45(4) (Winter), 853–86

McCarthy, John A. (1989), *Crossing Boundaries: History and Theory of Essay-Writing in Germany, 1690–1815*, Philadelphia, PA: University of Pennsylvania Press

McKinley, Mary B. (1994), 'The Essays as Intertext', *Approaches to Teaching Montaigne's Essays*, ed. Patrick Henry, New York, NY: MLA, 116–22

Meynell, Francis (1934), 'What Shall I Do in the Next War?', *Manifesto*, ed. C. E. M. Joad, London: George Allen & Unwin

Moi, Toril (1985), *Sexual/Textual Politics: Feminist Literary Theory*, London: Routledge

Montaigne, Michel de (1965), *The Complete Essays of Montaigne*, trans. Donald M. Frame, Stanford, CA: Stanford University Press

Newitt, Hilary (1937), *Women Must Choose*, London: Gollancz

Nussbaum, Martha (1996), *For Love of Country?*, ed. Joshua Cohen, Boston, MA: Beacon

Obaldia, Claire De (1995), *The Essayistic Spirit: Literature, Modern Criticism, and the Essay*, Oxford: Clarendon

Partridge, Eric [1948] (1970), *Words at War: Words at Peace*, Manchester, NH: Ayer

Pater, Walter [1983] (1912), *Plato and Platonism*, London: Macmillan

Peach, Linden (2000), *Virginia Woolf*, London: Palgrave Macmillan

Pleynet, Marcelin (1968), *Théorie d'ensemble*, Paris: Seuil

Poe, Danielle (2008), 'Replacing Just War Theory with an Ethics of Sexual Difference', *Hypatia* 23:2 (Apr.-Jun.), 33–47

Ponsonby, Arthur (1927), 'Disarmament by Example', speech by Mr. Arthur Ponsonby, M.P., in the House of Commons (17 Mar.), London: No More War Movement

—— [1927] (1991), *Falsehood in Wartime: Propaganda Lies of the First World War,* Costa Mesa: CA: Institute for Historical Review

Recchio, Thomas E. (1989), 'A Dialogic Approach to the Essay', *Essays on the Essay*, ed. Alexander J. Butrym, Athens, GA: University of Georgia Press, 272–88

Regosin, Richard L. (1994), 'The Essays: Autobiography and Self-Portraiture', *Approaches to Teaching Montaigne's Essays*, ed. Patrick Henry, New York, NY: MLA, 98–103

Renan, Ernest (1990), *Nation and Narration*, ed. Homi Bhabha, London: Routledge

Rettberg, Jill Walker (2008), *Blogging*, Cambridge: Polity

Rich, Frank (2006), 'So You Call This Breaking News?', *New York Times* (1 Oct.), Week in Review 10

Rosenbaum, S. P. (1992), *Women & Fiction: The Manuscript Versions of A Room of One's Own*, Oxford: Blackwell

Rosenman, Ellen Bayuk (1995), *A Room of One's Own: Women Writers and the Politics of Creativity*, New York, NY: Twayne Schaefer

Roy, Arundhati (2004), 'Do Turkeys Enjoy Thanksgiving?', *An Ordinary Person's Guide to Empire*, Boston, MA: South End Press

Scahill, Jeremy (2009), 'The Secret US War in Pakistan', *The Nation* (21/28 Dec.)

Schaefer, David L. (1994), 'Montaigne and Politics', in *Approaches to Teaching Montaigne's Essays*, ed. Patrick Henry, New York, NY: MLA, 69–77

Schenck, Celeste (1988), 'All of a Piece: Women's Poetry and Autobiography', *Life/Lines: Theorising Women's Autobiography*, ed. Bella Brodski and Celeste Schenck, Ithaca, NY: Cornell University Press

Schott, Robin May (2008), 'Just War and the Problem of Evil', *Hypatia* 23:2 (Apr.-Jun.), 122–40

Schwartz, Jerome (1994), 'Montaigne and Deconstruction', *Approaches to Teaching Montaigne's Essays*, ed. Patrick Henry, New York, NY: MLA, 131–7

Sears, Sallie (1983), 'Theater of War: Virginia Woolf's *Between the Acts*', in *Virginia Woolf: A Feminist Slant*, ed. Jane Marcus, Lincoln, NB: University of Nebraska

Sennett, Richard (1986), *The Fall of Public Man*, New York, NY: W. W. Norton

Silver, Brenda R. (1990), 'Cultural Critique', *The Gender of Modernism*, ed. Bonnie K. Scott, Bloomington, IN: Indiana University Press, 646–58

—— (1991), 'Textual Criticism as Feminist Practice', in *Representing Modernist Texts*, ed. George Bornstein, Ann Arbor, MI: University of Michigan Press

—— (1999), *Virginia Woolf, Icon*, Chicago, IL: University of Chicago Press

—— (1983), *Virginia Woolf's Reading Notebooks*, Princeton, NJ: Princeton University Press

Sontag, Susan (2001), [no title], *The New Yorker* (24 Sep). www.newyorker. com

Southworth, Helen (2005), '"Mixed Virginia": Reconciling the "Stigma of Nationality" and the Sting of Nostalgia in Virginia Woolf's Later Fiction', *Woolf Studies Annual* 11, 99–132

Stewart, Susan (1983), 'Shouts on the Street: Bakhtin's Anti-Linguistics', *Critical Inquiry* 10(2) (Dec.), 265–81

Tetel, Marcel (1990), *Montaigne*, Boston, MA: G. K. Hall

Tolstoy, Leo [1894] (1936), 'Christianity and Patriotism', in *The Kingdom of God and Peace Essays*, London: Oxford University Press

—— [1900] (2004), 'Patriotism and Government', *Anarchy Archives* (2 Jun.). http://dwardmac.pitzer.edu/anarchist_archives/bright/Tolstoy/patriotismand-govt.html

Tompkins, Jane P. (1980), *Reader-Response Criticism: From Formalism to Post-Structuralism*, Baltimore, MD: Johns Hopkins University Press

Vicinus, Martha (1972), *Suffer and Be Still*, Bloomington, IN: Indiana University Press

Watson, Julia (1994), 'En-gendering the Essays', *Approaches to Teaching Montaigne's Essays*, ed. Patrick Henry, New York, NY: MLA, 123–30

White, Hayden (1978), *Tropics of Discourse: Essays in Cultural Criticism*, Baltimore, MD: Johns Hopkins University Press

Willett, John [1932] (1964), *Brecht on Theatre: The Development of an Aesthetic*, New York, NY: Hill & Wang

—— (1967), *The Theatre of Bertolt Brecht: A Study from Eight Aspects*, London: Methuen

Woolf, Leonard (1963), *Beginning Again*, New York, NY: Harcourt Brace

Woolf, Virginia [1941] (1969), *Between the Acts*, New York, NY: Harcourt Brace Jovanovich

—— (1950), *The Captain's Death Bed and Other Essays*, New York, NY: Harcourt Brace Jovanovich

—— [1925] (1984), *The Common Reader: First Series*, ed. and intro. Andrew McNeillie, New York, NY: Harcourt Brace Jovanovich

—— [1932] (1986), *The Common Reader: Second Series*, ed. and intro. Andrew McNeillie, New York, NY: Harcourt Brace Jovanovich

—— [1942] (1970), *The Death of the Moth and Other Essays*, New York, NY: Harcourt Brace Jovanovich

—— (1977–84), *The Diary of Virginia Woolf*, ed. Anne Olivier Bell, 5 vols, New York, NY: Harcourt Brace Jovanovich

—— (1986-), *The Essays of Virginia Woolf*, ed. Andrew McNeillie, 4 vols, New York, NY: Harcourt Brace Jovanovich

—— [1958] (1975), *Granite and Rainbow*, New York, NY: Harcourt Brace Jovanovich

—— [1922] (1992), *Jacob's Room*, ed. and intro. Sue Roe, London: Penguin

—— (1975–80), *The Letters of Virginia Woolf*, ed. Nigel Nicolson and Joanne Trautmann, 6 vols, New York, NY: Harcourt Brace Jovanovich

—— (1982), *Melymbrosia. An Early Version of The Voyage Out*, ed. Louise A. DeSalvo, New York, NY: New York Public Library

—— [1947] (1974), *The Moment and Other Essays*, New York, NY: Harcourt Brace Jovanovich

—— (1976), *Moments of Being*, ed. Jeanne Schulkind, New York, NY: Harcourt Brace Jovanovich

—— ([1925] (1953), *Mrs Dalloway*, New York, NY: Harcourt Brace Jovanovich

—— [1919] (1992), *Night and Day*, ed. and intro. Julia Briggs, London: Penguin

—— [1928] (1933), *Orlando*, London: Hogarth

—— (1977), *The Pargiters*, ed. and intro. Mitchell A. Leaska, New York, NY: Harcourt Brace Jovanovich

—— (1990), *A Passionate Apprentice,* ed. Mitchell A. Leaska, New York, NY: Harcourt Brace Jovanovich

—— [1929] (1957), *A Room of One's Own*, New York, NY: Harcourt Brace Jovanovich

—— [1938] (1966), *Three Guineas*, New York, NY: Harcourt Brace & World

—— [1927] (1955), *To the Lighthouse*, Harcourt Brace

—— (1983), *Virginia Woolf's Reading Notebooks,* ed. Brenda R. Silver, Princeton, NJ: Princeton University Press

—— [1915] (1948), *The Voyage Out*, New York, NY: Harcourt Brace & World

—— [1931] (1959), *The Waves*, New York, NY: Harcourt, Brace & World

—— [1953] (1973), *A Writer's Diary*, ed. and intro. Leonard Woolf, New York, NY: Harcourt Brace Jovanovich

Zeller, Hans (1975), 'A New Approach to Critical Constitution of Literary Texts', *Studies in Bibliography* 28, 240–1

Zwerdling, Alex (1986), *Virginia Woolf and the Real World*, Berkeley, CA: University of California Press

Index